HISTORIC AMERICA

THE SOUTHWEST

Historic America

The Southwest

Brooks Robards

Thunder Bay
P·R·E·S·S
San Diego, California

Page 1: A spectacular vista across the Grand Canyon, Arizona.

Page 2: Racetrack Playa in California's parched Death Valley.

Thunder Bay Press
An imprint of the
Advantage Publishers Group
5880 Oberlin Drive
San Diego, CA 92121-4794
www.advantagebooksonline.com

ISBN 1-57145-560-4

Library of Congress Cataloging-in-Publication Data available upon request.

Printed in China
1 2 3 4 5 06 05 04 03 02

Acknowledgments and Photo Credits
The publisher would like to thank all who assisted in the production of this book, including those listed above, and: Deborah Hayes, for compiling the gazetteer and index; Debby Cooper; Simon Saunders. All color photographs in this volume are the copyright of Ed Cooper, unless otherwise noted by page number in the list below. Grateful acknowledgment is also made to the following individuals and institutions for permission to reproduce illustrations and photographs: © Larry Angier: 27, 124; © Mary Liz Austin: 32; © Ed Cooper, all color photographs in this volume except those listed separately here, and b/w images on pages: 59, 62r, 75, 114; © Terry Donnelly: 2, 7, 9, 14–15, 16–17, 20–21, 113, 115; © Carolyn Fox: 31, 108–09; © Rudi Holnsteiner: 19, 96, 105; © Stephen Trimble: 120–21; Artwork © Jeanne Walker Rorex: 68; Museum of New Mexico: 99, 119; Prints and Photographs Division, Library of Congress: 38, 42, 47, 50, 54, 58, 62l, 71, 72, 78 (both), 82, 83, 87, 90, 91, 94, 95, 98, 103, 106, 107, 110, 111, 115, 118, 123, 126, 127; National Archives: 46, 53, 63, 70, 86, 102, 122; Collection of Frank Oppel: 89; Saraband Image Library: 35, 51, 55, 67, 79; Yale University Map Collection, photograph © Joseph Szaszfai: 66

SERIES EDITOR: John S. Bowman
EDITOR: Sara Hunt
ASSOCIATE EDITOR: Robin Langley Sommer
PHOTOGRAPHY: Ed Cooper
ART DIRECTOR: Nikki L. Fesak
EDITORIAL ASSISTANT: Deborah Hayes

Table of Contents

INTRODUCTION

Page 6: Storm clouds gather over Jemez Canyon in northwest New Mexico. Jemez Pueblo in the Canyon served as a religious center in the 1630s.

Previous page: *Mission San Carlos in Carmel, California, was founded in 1769 by the Franciscan Father Junipero Serra. Originally in nearby Monterey, it was later moved. Father Serra established California's first library at the Mission.*

Opposite: *Snow festoons Mather Point on the south rim of the Grand Canyon in Arizona. Most visitors first view the Grand Canyon from this spot. It is located on Hermit Road across from the Canyon View Information Plaza.*

As the name of this great nation suggests, the United States of America consists of many individual parts with separate identities. Each of the millions of people who is "an American" belongs to a state, but also to a region. The borders of the nation as a whole, as well as of individual states, were once far more fluid than we think of them today. And to this day, in many ways these regions, of which the Southwest is only one, cohere even more distinctively than does the nation as a whole.

Think of the American Southwest and what comes to mind? Deserts and red-tinged mesas; oil rigs and cattle ranches; Mexican food and Spanish architecture; exotic gambling casinos and Native American adobe pueblos; old Western ghost towns and the glitter of Hollywood. Whatever associations we make, the region undeniably has its own unique flavor. Some would include Colorado and Arkansas as part of the Southwest. Others would exclude Texas as a land unto itself. Oklahoma is sometimes seen as sharing more with the culture of the Great Plains states. Stretching from Mexico up to Oregon, the state of California belongs geographically to the Northwest as well as the Southwest and really should be divided almost in half to fit these regional designations. Go to the atlas, and you will see that most of the Southwest region, including southern California, shares its southern border with Mexico. Add Nevada and Oklahoma to the four states that are contiguous with Mexico—California, Arizona, New Mexico, Texas—and you come up with a geographically cohesive region that is also culturally coherent. That is how you will find the Southwest defined in this book.

This designation of the region is certainly not the only one that has been used. As the new nation of the United States took shape in the eighteenth century, our Southwest was part of New Spain, and the "Old Southwest" signified a very different part of the country. Visionary though our founding forefathers may have been, they didn't look much past the Mississippi River. At that time, the region known as the Old Southwest included the lower portions of the Appalachian Mountains and the rivers near it that drain into the Atlantic and the Gulf of Mexico—what is now western Virginia, eastern Tennessee, Kentucky. Once North and South Carolina, along with Georgia, gave up their claims to sections of the Old Southwest adjacent to them, Congress created the Southwest Territory, which sent its own delegate to Congress. The regional borders moved westward with the pioneers, as citizens began to appreciate more fully that the United States would ultimately extend "from sea to shining sea."

From a geographical perspective, aridity and the desertlike topography that goes with it characterize the Southwest as we define it today. It was not always so. As we shall see, when the first human beings arrived in the Southwest, it had both a far wetter climate and a far more aqueous landscape. But the mountains that still entrance visitors have been there for millions of years, the result of a series of foldings and uplifts of land caused by the movements of the earth's plates. A series of these, for example, over millions of years, created what we know as the Rocky Mountains, which dip down into our Southwest in northern New Mexico, where a section is

THE SOUTHWEST

known as the San Juan Mountains. The Rockies form the Continental Divide, or Great Divide, which sends the waters of the nation's western rivers toward the Atlantic or the Pacific, depending upon which side they are on, and the snow and rain they accumulate feed most of the Southwest's watersheds. These include the Arkansas River in Oklahoma and the Rio Grande in New Mexico—both of which drain to the east—and the Colorado River, which drains westward as it runs through Arizona and along its borders with Nevada and southern California.

The Great Plains, another important geographic feature of the American West, includes most of Oklahoma, northern and western Texas, and eastern New Mexico. It marks the broad grasslands where buffalo grazed in the nineteenth century. The Great Plains also provided the routes west for fur traders and explorers along the Santa Fe Trail in the Southwest.

The Colorado Plateau, lying an average of 5,000 feet above sea level, reaches into northern Arizona and New Mexico, broken up by such volcanic cones as Arizona's San Francisco Mountains and New Mexico's Mount Taylor. Among the most sophisticated of the prehistoric Native American cultures, the Anasazi, precursors of the Pueblo Indians, made their home on the Colorado Plateau, apparently until severe droughts beginning in the twelfth century spurred them to move into the Rio Grande Valley.

The Plateau's most spectacular geologic feature is Arizona's Grand Canyon, the most magnificent of several canyons scattered along the Colorado River in the Southwest. These "inside-out mountains" run as deep as 5,000 feet. Native

Pages 10–11: Bright Angel Creek at the bottom of the Grand Canyon in Arizona displays some of the lush foliage typical of the area during springtime. The Creek joins the Colorado River not far from Phantom Ranch.

Left: Spring flowers beside a winding dirt road highlight the rugged beauty of Antelope Butte Reserve in Antelope Valley, Los Angeles County, California. The area is celebrated for its wild poppies and features 1,700 acres of California's official flower, the golden poppy.

Overleaf: Big Bend National Park in west Texas borders the Rio Grande and Mexico. Inhabited by prehistoric Native Americans for at least 10,000 years, the area has an abundance of plants native to the Chihuahuan Desert. An agave cactus, also called the century plant, is in the foreground; the Chisos Mountains, shown in the background, rise well over 7,000 feet.

Right: *Zabriskie Point in Death Valley, California, at dawn takes on the eerie look of an alien planet. It was named for borax mine superintendent Christian Zabriskie, and Italian film director Michelangelo Antonioni titled one of his films after it. In the background are the volcanic outcropping Manly Beacon and the Panamint Mountains. Only twelve miles wide, Death Valley extends for 130 miles.*

Americans, of course, had long known of the Grand Canyon, and the Spanish explored small segments in the sixteenth century. It was a U.S. Army expedition led by lieutenant Joseph Ives that made the first official survey in 1857; in 1869 John Wesley Powell made his epic 900-mile voyage down the Colorado River and through the Grand Canyon.

Physiographers refer to the section of the Southwest south and west of the Colorado Plateau as the Basin and Range Province. This very dry area features structural valleys, rather than those created by erosion, and includes California's Death Valley—at 280 feet below sea level the lowest point in North America—and the Salton Sea in the Imperial Valley. That portion of the Basin and Range Province that lies in Nevada is called the Great Basin because it has almost no exterior drainage. The other

portion consists of southern Arizona and New Mexico. In modern times, the natural water flow in this area and parts of the Colorado Plateau has been disrupted by the construction of dams—used for irrigation and power generation—that have caused major changes in the Southwest's natural environment.

The westernmost parts of the Southwest region fall into two geologic sections: the Sierra Nevada and the Pacific Border Province. The Sierra Nevada starts a mountain barrier that runs from southern California up through northern California, where it turns into the Cascade Range that runs all the way north into Canada. To the west of it, the Pacific Border Province includes California's Great Valley, which is bordered along the southwest by the Coast and Los Angeles Ranges. Southern California's coast is semiarid, and the com-

Above: *Indian blanket grows in front of a "dog-trot cabin" at the Lyndon Baines Johnson State Park in Stonewall, Texas. The colorful name for these double log cabins derives from the breezeway connecting them, which allows for cooler air to move through.*

Opposite: *Lichen form hieroglyphics on a rock near Wheeler Peak, which at more than 13,000 feet is Nevada's highest point.*

Previous pages: A field of Mexican poppies and Coulter's lupine blooms in Tonto National Forest north of Phoenix, Arizona, with the Superstition Mountains visible in the background. At more than three million acres, Tonto is one of the largest national forests.

bination of climate and a mountainous terrain leads to flooding, landslides, and mudflows during the winter rainy season. The San Gabriel Mountains to the north of Los Angeles, with elevations that are both steep and high, are particularly prone to the news-making land- and mudslides that destroy communities. A different kind of erosion plagues southern California's lowlands: stream erosion there causes arroyos that eat up land in urban developments.

Arid and desertlike as much of the Southwest may be, it produces many forms of vegetation, depending on the variety of ecosystems. In the earliest stages, grasslands dominated the region, from the central prairies and warm desert grasses of Texas, New Mexico, and Arizona to the shrub-steppes of Nevada and the grassy terrain of central California. Three types of grasses overspread the prairie sections of the Southwest— tall-grass, mixed-grass, and short-grass—depending on the amount of rainfall. Still abundant on the prairies are blanket flowers, sunflowers, coneflowers, goldenrod, and asters, depending on the season. Along the Continental Divide in New Mexico, plant life varies according to whether it grows on the eastern or western slope of the Divide. The southern Rockies provide habitat for both woodland and scrubland, featuring several varieties of oak, as well as juniper and Mexican piñon. Majestic ponderosa pine forests once covered northern Arizona and parts of New Mexico. In areas of the southern Rockies above the treeline, the tundra is filled with lichen, sedges, and other low-growing plants. Grasses, sedges, broad-leaved herbs, and hair grass inhabit the alpine meadows of the southern Rockies. In

southern California, the scrublands and woodlands that abound are part of the ecosystem known as "Mediterranean." Characterized by hot, dry summers and cool, wet winters, this ecosystem is found in only four other parts of the world. In the wettest parts of southern California are hardwood and needle-leaf evergreen forests, with oak and chaparral in the warmer, drier areas.

Most typical of the Southwest is the desert vegetation. It is found in the Great Basin of Nevada, and the Mojave, Sonoran, and Chihuahuan Deserts of both southern California and western Arizona. Sagebrush characterizes the Great Basin's vegetation, while the Joshua tree, creosote bush, and bur sage are common in the Mojave Desert of California. The saguaro cactus, staghorn, cholla, and barrel cactus live in the Sonoran Desert region of south-

ern California and southwest Arizona. In New Mexico and western Texas, near the Rio Grande and lower Pecos River Valley, mesquite grows, along with creosote bush, ocotillo, yucca, and the century plant. Salt marshes typify the coastal areas of the Pacific and the Gulf of Mexico, including cord grass, pickle weed, salt grass, rush, and sedge. One final Southwest ecosystem is located along southern California's coastline and is characterized by its woodlands of chaparral, oaks, laurel, madrona, golden chinquapin, and bayberry.

As distinctive as the Southwest's geography and vegetation is its animal life. In the early eras of the Southwest, many thousands of years before Christopher Columbus, but when human beings were already on the scene, many animal species—now extinct—roamed the region. Fossils have been found of

mammoths, camels, giant buffalo— more properly called bison—and king- sized beaver. The famous La Brea Tar Pits of Los Angeles contain these and still older fossils, including those of the saber-toothed cats, horses, and giant wolves, ground sloths, and bears. Scientists don't know exactly why these animals vanished, but overhunting by humans may have played a role. When the Spanish explorers first arrived in the Southwest, they found bison, pronghorn or antelope, American elk or wapiti, and bighorn sheep. In the days before settlers arrived, pronghorn were as numerous as bison. Even more abundant were deer, which provided Native American peoples with food, clothing, utensils, tools, and ornaments. The unlimited hunting that came with the expanding population of settlers almost annihilated some of the five species

Above: *White pelicans line up in the shallows of Salton Sea in California's Imperial Valley. This salty body of water is some 235 feet below sea level and was created when the Colorado River flooded an ancient, salt-covered depression in 1905, after construction of the Imperial Canal for irrigation purposes several years earlier.*

Opposite: Teddybear, or cholla, cacti (Opuntia bigelovii), frame Native American ruins at Tonto National Monument in Arizona near Theodore Roosevelt Lake. The teddybear cactus acquired its name because of its soft-looking, yellow-brown spines. The Salado tribe's masonry pueblo dates back 700 years.

of deer native to the Southwest. Conservation efforts eventually revived the mule deer, and the white-and black-tail varieties have recovered as well.

Among the Southwest's carnivores are wolves, coyotes, cougars, and, at one time, the grizzly bear, although that reclusive animal has steadily retreated north. One of our most familiar domesticated animals, the horse, had a major impact on the Southwest, particularly among its Native Americans. From early on, Spanish explorers brought horses with them, and inevitably, many escaped or were captured by Native Americans. The escapees ran wild and became known as "mustangs" (from a Spanish word for "stray animal"). As horses were acquired by native tribes, it became much easier to pursue bison and deer, and some groups shifted from farming to hunting exclusively.

At one time, small furbearing animals abounded in the Southwest. The region's trappers hunted primarily for beaver, but they also trapped mink, wolverine, marten, fisher, bobcat, lynx and, along the coastline of southern California, Pacific Ocean sea otter. Trapping was so extensive that many of these species were almost entirely wiped out. As the railroads extended their routes through the Southwest, professional hunters provided meat for the workers. The menu included bison, elk, sheep, and deer. Once the railroad lines were completed, meat and buffalo hides were shipped back East. The pattern of indiscriminate slaughter of these animals was repeated during the gold and silver rushes of the mid-1800s until, in the second half of the nineteenth century, the Southwest's wildlife population was decimated. The early settlers farming

in the prairie sections of the Southwest changed the habitat favorably, so that prairie chickens, grouse, and other game birds thrived. However, overhunting so reduced the bird and wildlife populations that by the turn of the century, the practice of banning hunting in national parks began.

President Theodore Roosevelt also began a series of national wildlife refuges in 1903, including some in the Southwest, and they soon grew into a nationwide network. The region's wolves, coyotes, jackrabbits, and prairie dogs continued to be hunted, but this time by federal agents. In the forefront of the national conservation movement at the turn of the century were two men: Gifford Pinchot and John Muir. Pinchot promoted the notion of "wise use," while Muir favored total protection for wildlife areas. By the 1940s and 1950s, the balance had tipped the other way, with some species, including deer, elk, and pronghorn, so prolific that herd management became necessary to protect slow-growing plantlife in the arid Southwest, as well as in other parts of the West.

Not all Southwestern animal species were indigenous. The ring-necked pheasant, imported from China in the 1880s, became a popular game bird in the region's prairie country. Other imported wildlife include Indian and African antelope, Barbary sheep, and several other species of Asian game birds. During the twentieth century, federal legislation helped support waterfowl refuges in the Southwest and in other parts of the nation, and it continues to promote ranching and farming practices that conserve wildlife habitat. A number of federal agencies have influenced wildlife management in the

Southwest. The mission of the Bureau of Land Management, established in 1946, includes wildlife conservation. So does the mandate of the Soil Conservation Service, begun in 1935. The Fish and Wildlife Service was developed in 1940 as part of the Department of the Interior with the express purpose of managing fish and wildlife resources.

Although the United States is often thought of as a young nation, the Southwest reminds everyone that the history of its people far predates not only the Declaration of Independence, but the arrival of the first Europeans. Native American culture in the region reflects patterns similar to those found in Mesoamerica, or Central America. New Mexico, for example, has been inhabited for at least 11,500 years, and possibly twice that long. Paleo-Indians left archaeological evidence of their cultures in northeastern New Mexico near Clovis, Folsom, and Sandia, as seen in chapter 1. The Cochise, part of what archaeologists identify as the Desert Culture, lived in southern New Mexico and Arizona approximately 8000 BC. The Mogollon people farmed in the valleys scattered along the New Mexico-Arizona border from 500 BC to AD 1200. Migrating north from Mexico were the Hohokam, or "vanished ones." They emerged as a distinct people only about the beginning of the modern era, and it was yet another century or so before the Anasazi people began to build their homes in the cliffs of northwestern New Mexico and Arizona. Pueblo peoples like the Hopi and the Zuñi are almost certainly descended from at least some of those earlier cultures, while the Navajo and Apache appeared in the Southwest much later.

The earliest populations inhabiting Oklahoma and Texas migrated there as part of a general movement into the Great Plains at the end of the Ice Age, some 12,000 years ago, in search of big game like mastodon and mammoth. In Texas, the Caddo farmed in the east; the Coahuiltecan lived to the south; Plains, or Lipan, Apache inhabited the west; and the Comanche and Tonkawa were in the north-central plains. Along the Gulf coast were Arkokisa, Attacapa, and Karankawa.

The most distinctive aspect of Native American culture in Oklahoma, which derives its name from the Choctaw words for "red people," concerns the removal of the so-called Five Civilized Tribes of the South to the eastern part of that state in the 1830s. The Cherokee, Choctaw, Creek, Chickasaw, and Seminole were forcibly removed from their homes and driven into Oklahoma, following what became known as the Trail of Tears.

California's Native Americans lived in greater isolation from each other than those in other parts of the Southwest because of that state's many mountains and deserts. The Mohave, Yuma, Kamia, Gabrielino, Serrano, Luiseño, and Dagueno tribes were among those who made their homes in the southern section of California that rightly belongs in the Southwest. They were among the 250,000 Indians living in more than 500 villages when the first non-native settlement was made there.

As much a part of "Anglo" North America as the Southwest may be today, it has a long tradition of Spanish influence. This began when the early Spanish conquistadors of the 1500s, including Francisco Coronado, initiated the influx of Europeans into the Southwest. In addition to discovering many regional

landmarks and mapping the area, the Spanish brought missionaries with them, who not only introduced Roman Catholicism, but also European settlements and farming practices. The Franciscan mission of San Diego de Alcalá, for example, dates back to 1769 and marks the starting point for El Camino Real, ("The Royal Road"), the first of California's major thoroughfares.

English and French explorers also came to the Southwest, although their influence was minor compared to that of the Spanish. The Louisiana Territory, purchased from France in 1803 and including sections of Texas and New Mexico as well as the entire state of Oklahoma, brought a large part of the Southwest under American control for the first time. The rest of the region remained in Spanish hands until Mex-

ico declared its independence from Spain in 1821, when it became a part of Mexico. Texas then broke away from Mexico and existed as an independent republic from 1836 to 1845. Not until the end of the Mexican-American War in 1848 did the Southwest begin to loosen its ties to Spain and Mexico, but Hispanic influence remains evident today in the prevalence of Spanish-language speakers. Such familiar words as "rodeo," "corral," and "lariat" are, in fact, imports. Mexican food, music, architecture, and art make up an important part of regional traditions. And not to be overlooked, as former Santa Fe journalist Hollis Engley points out, are the enclaves of Spanish-speaking families who trace their origins back to Spanish—not Mexican—occupation and still inhabit remoter sections of New Mexico.

Above: A full moon lights up San Xavier del Bac Mission near Tucson, Arizona. The mission was founded by Jesuit Eusebio Francisco Kino in 1692. After Charles III banned the Jesuit order from Spanish territories because of its secular activities, the mission was moved and the present building, constructed in 1783 in the late Baroque style of New Spain, was run by Franciscans.

Right: *The remains of a house that belonged to a branch of the John Doyle Lee family are situated at Lee's Ferry on the Colorado River, not far from the Grand Canyon in Arizona. Lee was the first to settle in the area. Lee's Ferry provided a natural crossing point from Utah to Arizona for Mormon settlers and was first used as such in 1864.*

Once the tumultuous years of war with Mexico were over, the Southwest, as we know it today, took shape. The Gadsden Purchase of 1853, besides replenishing Mexico's depleted coffers, added the southernmost strips of New Mexico and Arizona to the Southwest. Discovery of gold and silver just as the Mexican-American War was ending brought thousands of new settlers westward during the Gold Rush years. The region's economic and cultural growth were slowed in the 1860s by the Civil War, which divided loyalties. Some parts—Nevada, California—aligned themselves with the North, while others—Arizona, New Mexico, Texas—favored the Confederacy. Oklahoma was unaffiliated until a battle at Wilson's Creek, Missouri, pushed the Indian-dominated state into the Confederacy.

The economic identity of the Southwest took shape during the second half of the nineteenth century. While trapping, agriculture, and ranching attracted the earliest settlers to the area, their ranks were soon filled out by fishermen, miners, and workers in the burgeoning transportation, millwork, and oil-drilling industries. As these settlers and their occupations expanded, they impinged more widely on the lives and lands of the Native Americans. By the end of the nineteenth century, the native peoples had been "pacified" and confined to reservations, virtually obliterating their presence in the region's daily affairs except in colorful tourist meccas. During the twentieth century, however, Native Americans of the Southwest would revive their pride in, commitment to, and assertion of their own cultural traditions.

The important issues of the first half of the twentieth century revolved around

Above: A sign for Blacksmith General Store is one of the remnants of Mogollan, New Mexico, now a ghost town located in Gila National Forest. Mogollan was once New Mexico's leading mining town.

irrigation, hydroelectric power, mining, and oil-drilling technologies. With the advent of automobile and air travel, the Southwest ceased to be a remote, inaccessible region. Tourism developed into a booming industry, and Americans from all parts of the country, as well as from overseas, flocked to such national parks and monuments as the Grand Canyon, Walnut Canyon, Death Valley, Chaco Canyon, Lehman Caves, Bandelier, and the Carlsbad Caverns.

For those unacquainted with the Southwest's rich and complex past, the icons of American history may seem to reside almost exclusively on the East Coast. Those willing to explore more thoroughly will find here a multilayered cultural history reaching back thousands of years. The unique Southwest, as it unfolds in the following pages, helps complete the mosaic that makes the United States not only one of the world's greatest but most distinctive nations.

Left: *Center-city Los Angeles looms in the distance from Griffith Park Observatory on Mount Hollywood. A landmark since 1935, the Observatory and its planetarium receive two million visitors annually. The facility was donated by Col. Griffith J. Griffith, who studied mineralogy and made a fortune in Mexican mining.*

Overleaf: *Organ pipe and saguaro cacti stand silhouetted behind a field of Mexican gold poppies and blue lupine in Organ Pipe Cactus National Monument, Arizona. The organ pipe cactus was named for its many tubelike branches and is only found in this region of the Sonoran Desert.*

THE
FIRST
INHABITANTS

Previous page: The "White House" in the Canyon de Chelly, in northeastern Arizona, is the largest extant of some 100 cliff dwellings built by the Anasazi between about AD 350 and 1300.

When the first known human beings appeared in the region we are referring to as the Southwest, it would have been quite a different environment from that familiar not only to us today, but for all of the region's recorded history. It is generally accepted that they were descended from people who set out from Siberia—the first inhabitants of the Americas—who made their way across the land bridge known as Beringia, the dry floor of the shallow Bering Sea. If they came during the early stage of the Ice Age that began about 25,000 BC, they would have found an environment and climate totally different from today's. More likely, they came about 12,000 BC, as the great glaciers and ice sheets that covered all of North America down to the Ohio and Missouri Valleys had been receding for some millennia.

Even then, if the Southwest was a much damper and cooler region than it is in historical times, it would have been more temperate than the regions to the north. And it would have supported plentiful game for these first inhabitants, for they subsisted mainly by hunting large mammals—the mammoths, giant bison, llamas, camels, and others that then roamed these lands. Presumably that is why many of the oldest known finds indicating human presence in North America have been found in the Southwest. Not all the claims are generally accepted. Thus the materials found at Orogrande Cave, New Mexico, have been dated by their finder to at least 28,000 BC, but most of his fellow archaeologists are skeptical. Other similarly early finds that are disputed include those from sites near Calico, Yuma, San Diego, and Santa Rosa

Pages 36-37: The organ pipe cacti growing here are among the numerous unusual forms of plant and animal life to be found in the Organ Pipe Cactus National Monument, located in southern Arizona.

Island, California; Tule Springs, Nevada; Friesenhahn Cave in Texas; and Sandia Cave in New Mexico.

But there is no dispute about the finds from Clovis, east-central New Mexico, which are generally regarded as proof of the early presence of Paleo-Indians (prehistoric) in North America. These artifacts include finely flaked and fluted (grooved) stone points, usually made of obsidian or chalcedony, attached to spears or held as a knife and used to hunt and kill the mammoths, camel, ancient horses, and other big game. Such Clovis points (so named because they were first discovered at that site in New Mexico in 1929) were used throughout much of the Americas by at least 10,000 BC. The Clovis people were able to kill large animals because they launched their pointed spears with a hand-held wooden instrument known as the atlatl.

Some 1,000 years later, a slightly smaller projectile point was adopted by at least some Paleo-Indians, and again, the first discoveries were made in New Mexico—at Folsom, in 1926. The Folsom points were made of flint, and the Folsom people seem to have hunted mostly bison. But the earlier view that all of these first Americans lived almost entirely on the flesh of large mammals has been revised in more recent years. It is now believed that the diet of the Paleo-Indians of the Southwest included berries, nuts, fish, and other plants and animals. Analysis of human remains dated to about 9400 BC, found at Spirit Cave near Carson City, Nevada, show that the inhabitants apparently lived off freshwater fish and small mammals.

By about 6000 BC, the culture of the Indians of the Southwest had entered what anthropologists call the Archaic

Period. For one thing, the ice caps had thoroughly receded, and the climate was becoming much more like the one we know today: grassy plains and even deserts were replacing swamps and bogs. These Indians began to use a variety of materials for their tools and wares—bone and horn, leather, fibers for mats and baskets. Excavations at Danger and Lovelock Caves in Nevada reveal everything from baskets and nets to fur-cloth blanket fragments and leather sandals and moccasins. Other early Archaic sites in the Southwest include those around Lake Mohave and the Ventana Cave in Arizona, and Gypsum Cave in Nevada.

But perhaps the major difference is that the people were now shifting to a more vegetarian diet. Instead of pursuing large mammals, which for the most part had become extinct, they were gathering berries, seeds, and wild plants in more restricted areas; milling stones for grinding plants came into use. This meant that they were more settled, and, in fact, they would soon be practicing an early form of agriculture. The Southwestern peoples were among the first in North America to do so, which was undoubtedly due to their proximity to Mexico, where agriculture in the Americas appears to have started. Maize was evidently the first plant cultivated— about 5500 BC; the earliest traces in the present-day Southwest are those from Bat Cave, New Mexico, dated to about 1500 BC. Along with corn, squash and beans were also cultivated by this time:

Below: *This engraving depicting Florida Indians sowing maize and beans dates from the early sixteenth century, but archaeologists believe that Indians in the Southwest had been farming like this for thousands of years.*

Below: The crevasses and caves in the red sandstone walls of the Canyon de Chelly, located in northeastern Arizona, have sheltered Native Americans since AD 350. The canyon was designated a national monument in 1931. Navajo Indians still live and farm here.

these three plants would remain the staples of North American Indians' diet until modern times. Avocados and prickly pears were also among the earliest plants cultivated in the Southwest.

About 1300 BC several distinctive cultural traditions began to emerge in the region. These cultures are distinguished by such elements as food sources, pottery styles, technologies, and architecture, as well as by their religious ideas, social institutions, and political organizations. Southern California, for example, had been settled as early as any part of this region, first by hunters, then by seed-gatherers. One of the oldest known

groups is identified by its modern name, the Tipai-Ipai, who lived in Baja and southern California, from the coast inland to the Colorado River. The Yokuts of the southern San Joaquin Valley and the Chumash of the region just north of Los Angeles are other California tribes that can trace their ancestry far back. Eventually, California would be settled by scores of tribes who adapted to the diversity of the environments—deserts, seacoasts, forests, mountains, valleys. Two of the most distinctive characteristics of the California Indians were the baskets they made and the acorns they used as their dietary staple.

In Texas, tribes like the Caddo, the Tonkawa, and the Karankawas are probably also descendants of early Indians of the region. The Caddo were also found in Oklahoma. Whatever they called themselves, by 1300 BC the Indians of Texas and Oklahoma were beginning to show the same diversity in their means of subsistence, their material artifacts, and their cultural practices as were other tribes of the time. However, the most distinctive cultures that emerged in the Southwest are undeniably those centered in Arizona and New Mexico. The first of them, based in much of central and southern New Mexico, the southeastern corner of Arizona, and northwestern Texas, is named the Mogollon. The Mogollon people lived at first in shallow pit houses, with roofs pitched around a single center post. These homes were clustered in small groupings suggesting a close-knit community. Eventually the dwellings became more elaborate, as more rooms were added to form D-shaped apartmentlike dwellings. The Mogollon grew corn and other crops, but apparently these were ancillary food sources, since there was plenty of game in the forested mountains, grasslands, and streams around them.

The Mogollon are best known for their distinctive pottery. They seem to be the first of the Southwestern peoples to make pottery, beginning as early as 300 BC with plain brown and red earthenware. By about AD 700, they were decorating their pottery with painted designs. Several centuries later, one group of Mogollon, known as the Mimbres people, displayed both a craft and an art that attained new heights in painting red or black figures on white ground, or using several colors. They painted rather stylized insects, animals of all kinds, and humans engaged in various activities. It is not known for sure whether the subjects of this Mimbres pottery had some religious or spiritual significance; it is known, however, that when someone died, the Mimbres punched a hole in the bottom of a bowl and placed the vessel over the dead person's face to let the spirit out. The many examples of Mimbres pottery convey a good sense of this people's lives, yet the exact fate of the Mimbres and all Mogollon remains a mystery. The Mimbres pottery tradi-

Overleaf: These petroglyphs—carvings in stone—at Owens Valley, California, are among many carved by Indians throughout the Southwest. The exact age or significance of such carvings is usually not certain but many have some religious symbolism.

tion died out about AD 1200. The most widely accepted theory is that the Mogollon were absorbed into the Anasazi culture during droughts and migrations that occurred during the thirteenth and fourteenth centuries.

Long before this, about 300 BC, another culture had emerged in southeastern Arizona: the Hohokam. Their base was in the valleys of the Gila and Salt Rivers of the Sonora Desert. This was a more challenging environment, in which survival demanded water-supply management. The Hohokam constructed a system of canals to provide water both for drinking and for irrigating such crops as corn and cotton. Some of these canals stretched hundreds of miles; many of them remain. (It is said that the modern city of Phoenix copied some of this system when it built its modern water-supply works.) Unlike the Mogollon, the Hohokam scattered their homes with no apparent pattern.

The Hohokam also made fine painted pottery, but they developed something quite distinctive: they used the fermented juice of the cactus to etch sophisticated designs and figures in seashells (a technique that Europeans would not evolve for several centuries). The Hohokam people attained their peak about AD 1000 at such sites as Las Colinas and Snaketown, near Phoenix, and there another aspect of Hohokam culture emerges: the influence of the Mesoamerican culture to the south. Ball courts, platform mounds, shell jewelry, copper bells, parrot feathers, mir-

Above: *At El Morro National Monument, in western New Mexico, these are remains of an 875-room pueblo erected in the late thirteenth century AD. El Morro ("headland") rises 200 feet and has attracted visitors ever since the Spanish first saw it.*

Below: Pima Indians, depicted here, are most likely descendants of the Hohokam who once flourished in southeastern Arizona. The Pima were also among the first Indians in the Southwest visited by the early Spanish explorers.

rors, and anthropomorphic figurines all reflect some relatively close relationship between these Southwestern people and those of Mexico and Central America. What remains open to debate is whether these elements were passed on by direct contacts, including even large migrations, or whether they were simply products and ideas that were passed along by trade. In any case, the Hohokam are regarded as the ancestors of the Pima and Tohono O'odham peoples of historic times.

Perhaps the most dominant of these Southwestern cultures was that of the Anasazi or "Old Ones," which emerged about AD 700 in northwestern New Mexico and northeastern Arizona (and also in the adjacent lands of southeast Utah and southwest Colorado)—the area known today as the Four Corners. It is marked by sandstone plateaus, broad valleys, and narrow canyons. Like the land of the Hohokam, it is relatively arid, but instead of constructing irrigation canals, the Anasazi practiced "dry farming": rather than irrigating with quantities of water, they employed such techniques as minimizing water loss and soil erosion and developing drought-resistant varieties of plants.

The Anasazi are a somewhat mysterious people in that they were most likely related to their Mogollon and Hohokam neighbors, yet they came into their own somewhat later and eventually eclipsed, possibly even absorbed, the other two cultures. Yet the language they spoke is unknown: even their name, "Anasazi," is a Navajo word meaning "enemy ancestors." They began as nomadic hunters and foragers before settling down to raise a variety of crops. They tamed wild turkeys and, in addition to eating them, used their feathers to make robes. They also kept macaws as pets. The Anasazi excelled at fine basketry, but they also made pottery; some of the finest Native American pottery was the black-on-white Kayenta pottery with geometric designs. They used their region's rich turquoise deposits for making their own fine objects and for trading with the Indians of Mexico and California. They also carved and painted figures and signs on rocks like those at the Puye Cliffs in New Mexico.

But it is for their dwellings that the Anasazi would become most famous. Their first homes were partly underground and circular. They began to build above-ground granaries of mud-covered latticework, then of stone and mud mortar; then they began to live in above-ground dwellings, made sturdier with timber bracing. As they joined several of these with common walls, they evolved into apartmentlike, multistoried dwellings (ancestors of those that the Spanish would label pueblos—"villages"—centuries later). As the Anasazi expanded in population and power, their dwellings grew in size. The center of their far-flung culture was in the Chaco Canyon, in the Colorado Plateau of northwestern New Mexico. Along an eight-mile stretch were at least a dozen pueblos and major structures. The most prominent of these is the Pueblo Bonito, a crescent-shaped structure built circa AD 1050–100; with some 600 rooms, it probably accommodated about 1,000 people. Other grand Anasazi structures are to be found in Arizona's Canyon de Chelly and Tsegi Canyon.

Like all the Native Americans, much of Anasazi culture centered on religious beliefs and practices. A distinctive feature of the Anasazi was the kiva, a circular pit that was used for sacred ceremonies. Originally it would be underground and covered; later, kivas would be built within the pueblos. In the center of a kiva's floor was a sipapu, a hole that symbolized the entryway of their ancestors into this world. One of the most elaborate of all kivas is the one called Casa Rinconada, located in the Chaco Canyon. Perfectly round, it is 60 feet in diameter, and each axis is aligned to a cardinal point on the horizon; one of its windows allows a beam of sun-light to fall on a niche across the room on the day of summer solstice. The Anasazi were highly knowledgeable about the movements of the sun, moon, and stars, constructing calendars on which they based their crop planting.

Then, almost as suddenly as the Anasazi had appeared and flourished, they seem to have declined and vanished. Construction in the Chaco Canyon stopped about AD 1150. There are several theories. The most widely accepted one stresses the cycles of severe drought that struck the region beginning about this time. Contributing to the challenges this would have presented to their agriculture is the possibility that their over-farming had depleted the soil, and that cutting too much timber had destroyed the watersheds. Enemy tribes may have raided the prosperous Anasazi, but there is little indication of warfare, violence, or destruction. Whatever the cause, there began what is known as "The Great Migration," when between about 1150 and 1300, the Anasazi abandoned their major pueblos and appear to have wandered in various directions, mingling with other tribes, introducing some of their own beliefs and practices but also becoming absorbed by the indigenous peoples.

The Anasazi of the Kayenta region of northeastern Arizona, for instance, are believed to have mingled with Indians of the Black Mesa: together these people would become known in historic times as the Hopi. The Hopi were skilled agriculturists, using selective breeding and irrigation; they also painted their pottery and murals. They had their own villages, one of which—Oraibi, founded about AD 1200—is one of the oldest continuously inhabited communities in the United States.

Overleaf: The dwellings in the Gila Cliff National Monument in southwestern New Mexico date from about AD 1250-1350. The Indians erected their homes of stone, mud, and timbers in natural caves and crevasses in the cliff.

Right: Two young Mojave men, photographed by the famous nineteenth-century photographer Timothy O'Sullivan in the 1870s. Ancestors of the modern Mojave settled in the Mojave Valley in southern California about AD 1150.

The Anasazi also apparently moved into Mogollon territory in western New Mexico, resulting, it seems, in the emergence of the Zuñi people, centered in the many pueblos of the Zuñi Valley. Like their close relatives the Hopi, the Zuñi's religion stressed the role of kachinas (or katsinas)—the spirits that inhabited virtually everything in the natural world and acted as intermediaries between the spirit realm and the human world. Hopi and Zuñi men belonged to kachina societies that summoned the kachinas through the sipapu holes in their kivas; then the men appeared in elaborate masks and costumes to perform dances and songs. Imbued with the spirit of the kachinas they represented, the dancers gave kachina dolls to the children. Carved from cottonwood root and brightly painted and decorated, these dolls were not toys, but were designed to instill respect for tribal religion and discipline in behavior.

By about the year 1500, there were an estimated 250,000 people living in pueblos stretching from the Rio Grande Valley in northern New Mexico over to the mesas of northeastern Arizona. Sharing many cultural traditions, although not all spoke the same languages, they lived in peaceful coexistence. But for at least a century or more, groups of new tribes had begun to appear among them. Coming from the north, these nomadic strangers did not speak a language anything like those of the Pueblo Indians. These newcomers also brought different cultural traditions: they dressed in animal skins, used dogs as pack animals, and lived in tent-like houses made of brush or hide. In fact, their original homeland was in the northwestern Canadian subarctic, and they spoke an Athapaskan language based in that region. They called themselves Diné, or Ndee, "The People."

At first the Diné settled in the mountains on the fringes of the Pueblo Indians' territory, and what they could not provide for themselves, they acquired by barter. But some of them, accustomed to a more vigorous life of hunting bison, were a more aggressive people who sporadically raided the pueblos for food, weapons, women,

children, or other booty. For this reason, these Indians would eventually become known as "Apache," a Zuñi word for "enemy." They remained a fairly nomadic people who lived by hunting and foraging, and they were organized only in relatively small extended-family groups. Some of the Apache eventually spread out well into Texas and western Kansas.

Other groups of these newcomers eventually began to adopt many of the Pueblo Indians' habits, arts, and customs; in particular, they settled down to farming, and became known as "Navajo," a Tewa word for "planted fields." The Navajo even changed from wearing their traditional buckskin clothing to adopting the cotton shirts and blankets of the Pueblo Indians. Eventually they would adopt many

Below: These Hopi Indians are performing a ceremony at the sacred spring at the Second, or Middle, Mesa, in northeastern Arizona. The Hopi organize much of their life and routine around religious ceremonies.

Pueblo religious beliefs and rituals as well. For example, they took the Pueblos' basic technique of sand-painting and developed it into a sophisticated art used in healing and other ceremonies.

However, many of the elements that would come to distinguish the cultures of the Navajo, Apache, and other tribes throughout the Southwest in historic times did not emerge until well after 1500. And before that process could take place—and indeed, helping to shape that process—there occurred the cultural equivalent of the meteor that left the great crater near Flagstaff, Arizona. It was the appearance of the Europeans.

Right: *This hogan (from the Navajo name,* hoogan), *in Navajo National Monument in northeastern Arizona, is typical of the early Navajo dwellings. Like all hogans, its entrance faces east.*

EXPLORATION
AND
EARLY SETTLEMENTS

Above: *Spain's King Ferdinand points across the Atlantic to the New World in an engraving dating from 1493, the year after Columbus reached the Americas.*

From the arrival of Christopher Columbus's ships in the West Indies in 1492, Spain dominated early investigations of the southern regions of the New World. No wonder, then, that it was Spaniards, or those who sailed on their behalf, who discovered and explored the coast and interior of the Southwest.

In 1519, six years after Vasco Nuñez de Balboa discovered the Pacific Ocean, a less celebrated Spanish explorer, Jamaica's Governor Alonso Alvarez de Piñeda, began a nine-year voyage through the Gulf of Mexico. His maps include the first chart of the Texas coast. Then, in 1528, the nobleman Álvar Núñez Cabeza de Vaca found himself stranded on the Texas coast near Galveston, along with Alonso de Castillo and Andres Dorantes, with his Moorish slave Esteban de Dorantes. The four had been part of a large Florida *entrada*, or entry, as the Spanish conquistadors called their quasi-military expeditions into the New World interior. They spent some eight years wandering among the native peoples before meeting with a party of Spanish raiders near the Pacific Coast of northern Mexico. Cabeza de Vaca regaled the viceroy of New Spain, as the Spanish-occupied Mexico was called, with stories of gold-laden cities in what is now the American Southwest, and the legend of the Seven Golden Cities of Cibola was born. (Cibola seems to have been a Zuñi word for their region.)

No longer a slave, Esteban apparently believed that he now was regarded as a shaman by the Native Americans he encountered during his wanderings. He served as a guide for a second exploratory expedition (1539), headed this time by Franciscan missionary Marcos de Niza. Following the ancient turquoise trail and the Sonora and San Pedro Rivers, Esteban reached what he believed was the first city of the mythical Cibola. In fact, it was Hawikuh Pueblo in northern New Mexico, and whatever happened next, he was killed by the resident Zuñi. Niza, the first European to set foot in Arizona, apparently never glimpsed the so-called magical city, but simply claimed the region for Spain and returned to Mexico. Nevertheless, he reported to Francisco Vázquez de Coronado, governor of New Galicia, a frontier of New Spain, on its fabulous wealth.

The twenty-nine-year-old Coronado was chosen to lead a new *entrada* into what was now mistakenly believed to be El Dorado, the legendary New-World city based on Peruvian mythology and ruled by a leader who was dusted with gold. Arrayed in his gleaming armor, Coronado led a force of more than 300 Spaniards and European mercenaries. They left Compostela, Mexico, on February 22, 1540. Some 700 Mexican Indians accompanied them as guides and servants. The expedition traveled with more than 200 horses and herds of sheep and cattle. Support ships commanded by Hernando de Alarcón were to travel up the Pacific Coast to supply Coronado and his entourage. This New World crusade included women and children, and Father Marcos de Niza led a contingent of Franciscan missionaries assigned to convert the natives. It was the last great *entrada* of the Spanish conquistadors.

Captain Melchior Díaz, sent ahead to reconnoiter the mythical Cibola, reported to Coronado that the city did not exist. Moreover, the unfriendly Hawikah Zuñi still had Esteban's bones on display. Undeterred, on April 22, 1540, Coronado sent ahead an advance party of some 100 conquistadors with Indian support. After a friendly reception at Corazones, a settlement named for the 600 deer hearts offered to Esteban and Cabeza de Vaca on their earlier expedition, the party pressed on. Traveling up the Sonora River, they entered what is now the United States near Palominas, Arizona. Their path took them along the San Pedro and Gila Rivers to Sonora Desert country (centuries later, the setting for many famous Western movies).

The Mogollon Plateau forests of Arizona's Black River basin provided welcome but temporary relief. The Colorado Plateau lay before them, and Coronado sent ahead García Lopez de

Page 49: Mooney Falls on the Havasupai Indian Reservation, Grand Canyon, Arizona—unknown to outsiders before the sixteenth century. The falls drop 190 feet and feature a series of tunnels.

Left: A sixteenth-century engraving illustrates how Native Americans extracted gold from rivers in the Southwest for the Spanish.

Cárdenas as a scout. Zuñi warriors ambushed Cárdenas's camp near the Zuñi River in the earliest Native American-European skirmish of the Southwest. By the time Cárdenas reached the mythical Cibola—actually Hawikuh—Coronado had joined him. On July 7, 1540, Zuñi forces drew a battle line of corn meal in front of their pueblo. The superior Spanish weaponry routed the defenders, who had never seen horses before. The first city of Cibola was conquered, but it was not what Father Niza had led Coronado to believe. The city had no gold, silver, or turquoise. Indeed, its architecture was impressive, and the Spaniards' consolation was an excellent store of food. In letters to his viceroy, Coronado described the Zuñi as an intelligent people. "There are many animals here," he added, listing bears, bobcats, cougars, porcupines, elk, goats, peccaries, deer, and buffalo. Unwilling to abandon the *entrada*, Coronado resolved to continue the search for gold. His sorties represent the first significant exploration in the history of the Southwest.

Learning from the Zuñi about Tusayan, supposedly an affluent province northwest of Hawikuh, Coronado sent Pedro de Tovar, Father Juan de Padilla, and a band of soldiers to investigate. Zuñi guides led the group over an ancient Native American trade route past Navajo Springs, the Petrified Forest, and the Jeddito Valley. At Awatowi Pueblo near Antelope Mesa, the party engaged Hopi

Below: The Spanish-Franciscan mission of San Geronimo near Taos Pueblo, New Mexico, was built in the seventeenth century and was one of the earliest in the New World. It is a World Heritage site.

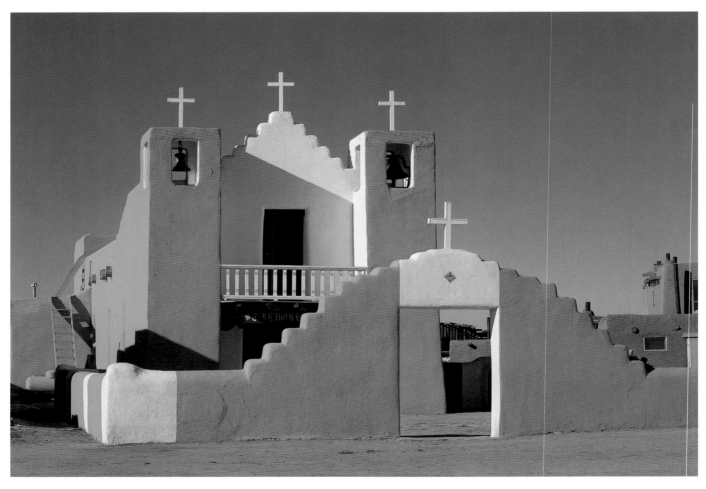

Left: Coronado, one of the most famous of the Spanish conquistadors, left Compostela, Mexico, for Gran Quivira in 1540. It was the last major Spanish entrada ("entrance"), or expedition, in the Southwest.

warriors. No match for the mounted Spaniards, the Hopi sued for peace. Traveling across Black Mesa, Tovar's group visited Walpi, Mishongnovi, Shongopovi, and Oraibi Pueblos—the latter believed to be one of the oldest continually inhabited towns on the continent—but still could find no gold.

The year before, in 1539, another Spanish adventurer, one Francisco de Ulloa, had explored Mexico's Gulf of California and most likely passed the mouth of the Colorado River. Then he left the gulf and proceeded along the Pacific coast of California, perhaps as far north as what is now San Diego. The Gulf of California and Baja (or Lower) California, in fact, had been discovered in 1533 by Fortún Jiménez, a Basque pilot sailing for the Spanish in Mexico, who thus became the first European to reach the southernmost limits of California. But Jiménez believed Baja California was an island, so Ulloa is credited with idenifying it as a penin-

sula. However, the honor of being the first European to view the California coast usually goes to Juan Rodriguez Cabrillo, a Portuguese explorer in the service of Spain who arrived in 1542. Cabrillo first visited Catalina Island and Santa Barbara Channel, then sailed north of San Francisco as far as Point Reyes. When he died in 1543, his men continued their expedition under the leadership of Bartolomé Ferrelo, traveling past Cape Mendocino to Oregon.

Aware of Ulloa's 1539 report of a river that entered the Gulf of California, Coronado speculated that it might be the great river described by the Hopi. He sent Garcia Lopez de Cárdenas and twenty-five cavalry in search of the river, hoping his envoy might also be able to liaise with the supply ships captained by Alarcón. They crossed the Coconino Plateau and found themselves before a natural wonder that left them speechless. They had discovered the Grand Canyon. Far below, the

Above: *A nineteenth-century photo of Hopi village ruins. The Hopi culture emerged about 800 years ago in what is now Arizona. Their reservation today encompasses parts of Navajo and Coconino Counties in northeast Arizona.*

Colorado River was looking, from that height, like a trickle. In vain, Cárdenas sought a way to cross the gigantic chasm before he had to return to Hawikuh.

At Corazones, the bulk of Coronado's forces had established a base camp headed up by Tristan de Arellano. Coronado decided to send his scout Melchior Díaz south to Corazones with orders for Arellano to break camp and join Coronado at Hawikuh. Then Díaz was to travel southwest to the Pacific in hopes of finding Alarcón's supply fleet. Díaz and two dozen mounted men headed through Pima and Papago country, possibly traveling along the Camino del Diablo, or Devil's Highway.

Following the lower Colorado River, Díaz discovered a message carved in a tree on the riverbank: "Alarcón came this far." Letters buried at the foot of the tree told Díaz he had missed the seaman by two months. In fact, Alarcón had been the first European to explore the Colorado River, using two small boats and some twenty men. On his second venture he reached the vicinity of Fort Yuma, above the junction with the Gila River. There he erected a cross and hid the letters later found by Coronado's men. Pressing on, Díaz and his party crossed the river on rafts and entered the Mojave Desert, becoming the first Europeans to enter present-day California from the east.

That same year, 1540, Coronado dispatched another expedition under Hernando de Alvarado to explore the lands to the east. Leaving the Hawikuh Pueblo, Alvarado and his men became the first Europeans to see, atop a high mesa, Acoma, the oldest continuously inhabited town in the United States. In September they also became the first Europeans to reach the Rio Grande, named by Alvarado Río de Nuestra Señora ("River of Our Lady").

One of Alvarado's Indian guides had been spinning tall tales about the riches to be found in Quivira, northwest of the Tiguex settlements in New Mexico where Coronado had established his new camp. Motivated by gold lust, Coronado's forces cruelly mistreated their Indian hosts in an effort to extract more information. The rape of a Tiguex woman led to outright war, and the conquistadors went on a rampage notorious for its brutality, running down some Tiwas Indians on horseback, burning others alive, and destroying twelve pueblos. Emerging on the endlessly flat Great Plains, Coronado saw "not a stone, not a bit of rising ground, not a tree, not a shrub, not anything." The conquistadors encountered massive herds of buffalo and began the slaughter that would lead to the animals' near extinction by the end of the nineteenth century.

Before Coronado and his officers finished their search for the gold of Quivira, they had explored not only New Mexico and Arizona, but also parts of Texas, Oklahoma, and Kansas. In this last region they found the thatched-roofed huts of Quivira but no gold; Quivira was, in fact, a simple pueblo of the Wichita. After suffering a head injury in an informal horse race, Coronado was carried home on a litter. Many of his men blamed him for the failure to find gold. Once he resumed governorship of New Galicia, he underwent an inquisition and was fined and stripped of his position. His rival Hernando de Soto, who had wandered the wilds of Florida and discovered the Mississippi River in 1541, is likely to have ventured as far as the eastern boundary of the Southwest, in Arkansas. During the next five decades, only Spain's Franciscan missionaries returned to the Southwest interior, happy to mine the spiritual gold of its deserts, mesas, plains, and canyons by attempting to bring Christianity to the natives.

When Coronado and his forces left Cicuye, east of Santa Fe, one of the Franciscan missionaries who stayed behind to proselytize was Father Luis de Ubeda. With him was a young black companion, Cristobal, whom he hoped could help him by learning Indian dialects. Both men were probably murdered by avenging natives, soon after

Coronado and his men left the area in 1542. Father Juan de Padilla also stayed behind to found a mission at Quivira, and became the first Roman Catholic martyr in the region when he was killed by a party of Sioux warriors.

During his round-the-world voyage, England's Francis Drake sailed up the Pacific Coast in 1579. Making landfall near San Francisco Bay, he dubbed the region New Albion and claimed it for England. News of this rival nation's claim helped spur the Spanish to renew their Southwestern explorations in 1581. That same year, three Franciscan missionaries traveled north through El Paso, Texas: Francisco Sanchez Chamuscado, Augustin Rodriguez, and Juan de Santa Maria. The first Europeans to sail up the Rio Grande, all three died before their mission was completed. Hernán Gallegos guided the rest of the entourage back to Mexico. In 1582 Antonio de Espejo and Father Bernardino Beltran retraced the missionaries' route, discovering that they had all been murdered by the Tiguex.

Overleaf: The Grand Canyon from the South Rim, near Bright Angel trailhead. Dispatched by Coronado, Cardenas was the first Spaniard to view the Grand Canyon.

Below: Spanish brutality to Southwestern natives was notorious, driving some Native Americans to suicide, as depicted in this sixteenth-century engraving.

Although Beltran eventually returned home, Espejo followed the Pecos River and traveled into Arizona. Espejo's forays probably did more to spur Hispanic settlement of New Mexico than those of any other early explorer.

Not all the explorations were sanctioned by the Spanish colonial government. In 1590 Gaspar Castaño de Sosa organized the first non-government expedition into New Mexico. He crossed the Pecos River Valley in south Texas with the first wagon train to enter future U.S. territory. In 1594 Francisco Leyva de Bonilla spent a year illegally exploring among the upper Rio Grande native communities. Shortly after his expedition arrived in Quivira, Kansas, Bonilla's second in command, Antonio Gutierrez de Humana, murdered him and took over. Some historians believe that Humana reached the Mississippi River before retracing his steps

and dying at the hands of Indians, although nothing of the party's final outcome is known for certain.

In 1598 Juan Zaldivar de Oñate, scion of a silver-mining family, founded the first permanent settlement in New Mexico near the Chamas River, north of Albuquerque. He called it San Juan de los Caballeros. When Oñate's treatment of the Acoma Pueblo inhabitants provoked a revolt in 1599, he quashed it with a killing spree. Oñate served as the first governor of New Mexico, but after eight years, he was recalled and put on trial, much like Coronado. Oñate's replacement, Pedro de Peralta, moved the little town south after his appointment in 1610 and renamed it La Villa Real de Santa Fe de San Francisco ("The Royal City of the Holy Faith of St. Francis"). This town would become the largest Spanish settlement in New Mexico.

Below: *This old photo shows one of the many Franciscan missions in New Mexico. Friar Marcos de Niza is considered to have established the earliest one, near Zuñi pueblo, in 1539.*

Several Spanish navigators landed in southern California at the turn of the sixteenth and seventeenth centuries. In 1587, traveling from Macao, China, to Acapulco, Captain Pedro de Unamuno anchored at Morro Bay City, which he named Puerto de San Lucas (near today's San Luis Obispo). He led a party of men ashore, and a day later they were attacked by Indians, who murdered one of the invaders and wounded four; Spanish gunfire killed some of the attackers. Sebastian Vizcaíno received approval from the Spanish colonial viceroy to explore California and did so in 1602–3, discovering Monterey Bay.

By 1626 New Mexico had forty-three Franciscan missions from Pecos to Acoma and Taos to El Paso del Norte. Some were small outposts, while others were population centers, including Pueblo de las Humanas in the Gran Quivira National Monument site. The remains of a grand Franciscan church in Cicuye, east of Santa Fe, lie in Pecos National Monument. Despite the often good intentions of the Spanish explorers and the missionaries who followed them in New Mexico, the impact of their presence on native life was detrimental. The colonials treated the Indians like a conquered people, plundering their crops, raiding their pueblos, and using them as slaves. European diseases including smallpox, measles, syphilis, and cholera led to epidemics that decimated a vulnerable local population.

Although they lacked their oppressors' superior weaponry, many tribes still attempted to resist colonial domination. Gradually they acquired expertise in horsemanship, on stolen or strayed Spanish steeds. In the 1680 uprising called the Pueblo Revolt, led

by a San Juan medicine man known as Popé, Spanish colonists were killed and driven out of Santa Fe. They retreated to El Paso, where they built Texas's first two missions, and did not return to Santa Fe for twelve years. In present-day Arizona, Jesuit missionary Eusebio Francisco Kino established twenty-four missions, converting the native people to Christianity and European farming methods. This Renaissance man made fifty expeditions during his twenty-four years in the Southwest and raised cattle on twenty ranches to feed his Indian converts. One mission, San Xavier del Bac, founded in 1700, still exists near Tucson. The Spaniard Francisco Cuervo y Valdes founded Albuquerque in 1706. Then Spanish military forces built a fort at Tubac in 1752 to protect colonial interests. When the king, Charles III, expelled the Jesuits, Franciscan missionaries including Fathers Juan Díaz and Francisco Garcés took over.

New World exploration fever was not confined to the Spanish and the English. René Robert Cavelier, Sieur de La Salle,

Above: *Inscription Rock, El Morro National Monument, New Mexico, reads in Spanish: "Passed here Governor Don Juan de Oñate from discovery of the Sea of the South [Gulf of California] on the 16th of April 1605." Oñate probably did not reach the Gulf of California.*

who started off in New France, as eastern Canada was then known, decided to move south and west to look for the Pacific Ocean. In 1582 when he arrived in the territory known as Louisiana, it included the present-day Oklahoma, and La Salle claimed the entire region for France. Although he did not set foot in Oklahoma, other French explorers and traders did, soon after his claim. When La Salle reached Texas via Matagorda Bay, he built Fort Saint Louis. On an expedition from the fort in 1687, he was killed by his own men, and the fort was destroyed by natives two years later. Hearing about the French incursion, Spanish explorer Alonso de Leon left for Fort Saint Louis in 1689 with plans to attack. Finding it already destroyed, they continued to the Neches River. Traveling with Leon was a Franciscan who established San Francisco de los Tejas, the first mission in east Texas, in 1690.

Diego de Vargas, who had become governor of the region, re-established Spanish control of New Mexico in 1692. Peace with the natives remained tenuous, though, and the pueblos of Tewa, Tano, and Tiwa staged an uprising in 1696, suppressed harshly by the Spanish. The conquistadors extended their reach into Texas by setting up missions west of the Rio Grande in 1703. By 1716 four more Spanish missions had been established near the Neches and Angelina Rivers, and East Texas had been reclaimed for Spain. The Alamo, built in 1722 as a Franciscan mission, eventually was incorporated into the Spanish fort there.

By 1760 traders were beginning to extend Spain's reach into Nevada's Great Basin, but Francisco Garcés is considered the first European to enter

Left: *San Xavier del Bac Mission lies nine miles south of Tucson. Its architecture exemplifies New Spain's late Baroque style.*

Below, right: The bell at San Juan Capistrano. Named for a fourteenth-century Italian theologian, the Orange County mission is considered the oldest church in California.

Below: The Alamo Mission in San Antonio, site of the 1836 massacre of Texans including Davy Crockett, is visited by 2.5 million tourists annually.

the territory in 1776, during his travels between New Mexico and California. Meanwhile, the explorations of two more intrepid Franciscan missionaries, Francisco Dominguez and Silvestre Velez de Escalante, traveled even farther north into present-day Colorado and Utah. Several settlements and points of interest in this region are named for Escalante, including the town of Escalante, Utah.

The Spanish had made more than ninety forays through Texas by 1731, leaving their mark in the form of forts and missions. San Antonio de Bexar, the fort built in 1718 to protect San Antonio de Valero Mission, ultimately grew into the modern city of San Antonio. In 1772 this settlement became the capital of the Spanish province of Texas.

Although the French played a less important role in the exploration of the Southwest than the Spanish, their presence in the Louisiana Territory was an important factor and encouraged excursions west. Pierre and Paul Mallet entered New Mexico in 1739. In the case of the vast Louisiana Territory, the Spanish explorer Hernando de Soto had claimed it in 1541, but La Salle superseded that claim for France in 1582. The French established the first permanent settlement in the Louisiana Territory at Fort St. Jean Baptiste, or Natchitoches, in 1714. France ceded Louisiana, including Oklahoma, back to Spain in 1762, but Spain returned the territory to France in 1800.

Spanish exploration of California also continued. Baja California's governor, Gaspar de Portola, traveled north to San Diego and built the first fort, or *presidio*, there in 1769. He built a second in 1770 at Monterey. Accompanying him was Franciscan missionary Junipero Serra, who founded the first San Diego mission in 1770. Appointed the *padre presidente* of California, Serro quickly established nine more missions, including those at Santa Barbara, San Luis Rey, and San Francisco de Asis. The latter, begun in 1769, was finished in 1791 and is known today as Mission Dolores (and still appreciated by all who visit San Francisco). San Jose Mission was built

Left: Children of Spanish origin pose outside a New Mexico adobe church in a photo taken at the turn of the twentieth century. Many elements of the Spanish and Native American cultures merged in this region.

in 1797, twenty years after the founding of nearby San Jose Pueblo as the first secular community in Spanish California. San Juan Capistrano was started in 1776, but the main church there was not built until 1797. Each mission was a one-day walk from another, along a route that became known as the Camino Real ("royal highway"). By 1823 the Franciscans had established a total of twenty-one missions in California.

Both Francisco Garcés and Juan Bautista de Anza contributed to the exploration of southern California in the late eighteenth century. Garcés inscribed a rock in the Mojave Desert near California City during his travels in 1774. De Anza was charged with the task of opening up a supply route to Mexico and founded a *presidio*, at Yerba Buena, which later became San Francisco, in 1776. He also explored

the San Luis Valley and the Arkansas River before returning to New Mexico. Tucson, Arizona, was established, initially as a fort, in 1776.

The long era of European colonization in the Southwest came to a close in 1803, when the United States bought the Louisiana Territory from France for $15 million. Included in the purchase were parts of the Southwest including all of Oklahoma and parts of Texas and New Mexico. Stretching from the Mississippi River across to the Rocky Mountains and from the Gulf of Mexico to Canada, this vast region included all or most of thirteen future states, which is why it has been called the greatest real-estate deal in history. Its acquisition by the fledgling nation called the United States of America ushered in a new period in the life and culture of the Southwest.

Overleaf: San Diego de Alcala garden. This California mission was built in 1769 by Father Junipera Serra.

FORGING
THEIR
DESTINIES

Previous page: *The Rio Grande, near Questa, New Mexico, is now managed by the National Parks Service as part of the National Scenic and Wild River area.*

Below: *Detail of John Mitchell's map of the Louisiana Territory from 1755, when it was still owned by France.*

While the long era of Southwestern exploration by the Spanish had ended by the beginning of the nineteenth century, Spain continued to exert influence in the region. It did, after all, still possess what would become the U.S. states of California, Nevada, Texas, Utah, Arizona, and New Mexico as well as portions of Wyoming, Colorado, and Oklahoma. Unlike the Americans, the Spanish were more interested in exploiting such natural resources as gold and converting the Native Americans than they were in colonizing the lands they

controlled. As the nineteenth century proceeded, tension grew inexorably between the United States and Spain over its holdings all across the southern band of North America.

This tension turned into outright war in 1818, during the administration of President James Monroe, when Andrew Jackson invaded Spanish-held Florida. In the negotiations that followed this episode, Monroe's secretary of state, John Quincy Adams, proved a tough negotiator with the Spanish ambassador to the United States, Luis de Onis, and

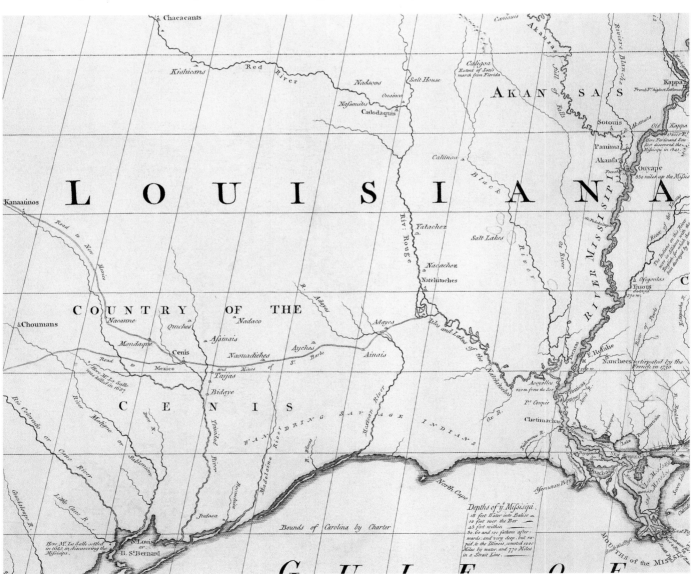

insisted upon defining more strictly Spain's vague borders with his nation. In the Adams-Onis Treaty of 1819, although Adams persuaded Spain to yield Florida to the United States, he settled for a Spanish-American border at the Sabine River, today the western boundary of the state of Louisiana. That meant giving Texas to Spain, a concession that would later come back to haunt Adams politically. The third component of the Adams-Onis Treaty clarified the westernmost boundaries of the 1803 Louisiana Purchase, something that had not been done at the time the historic agreement was concluded.

Adams made sure the boundary extended to the Pacific Ocean at the 42nd parallel, which helped in a later dispute over the Oregon Territory. Oklahoma's panhandle, however, went to Spain. The remainder of present-day Oklahoma became part of the new Arkansas Territory, created in 1819. Its first settlers moved into such towns as Miller Court House, Salina, and Three Forks soon after. Expeditions by U.S. Army officers, who included James B. Wilkinson, George C. Sibley, J. R. Bell, Stephen H. Long, and Hugh Long, provide the earliest nineteenth-century records for Oklahoma.

During the second quarter of the nineteenth century, the U.S. government began forcing Native American tribes in the Southeast to relocate across the Mississippi River in order to make room for American settlers. The Five Civilized Tribes, as the Chickasaw, Cherokee, Choctaw, Seminole, and Creek were called (a term that has fallen into disfavor among many historians), were pressured into signing treaties that provided for their relocation into eastern Oklahoma, which was known as Indian Territory.

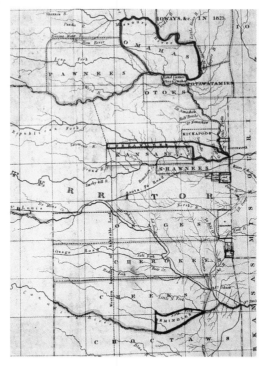

Left: An early map of Indian Territory, as much of Oklahoma was once called, shows Osage, Cherokee, Creek, Seminole, and Choctaw land allotments.

The government constructed two forts to supervise and protect the relocated Native American population. Fort Gibson, at the confluence of the Grand, Arkansas, and Verdigris Rivers, had been singled out in 1806 as a likely spot for a garrison by Wilkinson when he explored the Arkansas River. Built in 1824, it became the center of military operations for the entire Indian Territory. Fort Towson was built the same year to protect the Choctaw from outlaws in the Red River area and Plains Indian raiders.

The relocation of the Five Civilized Tribes proceeded over two decades, from 1819 to 1839. Under duress, each tribe beat a path from its home in the Southeast—Georgia, Tennessee, Alabama, Florida—that became known collectively as the Trail of Tears. The names of many Oklahoma towns reflect this period. Wetumka, north of the Canadian River in eastern Oklahoma, was so named because in Creek dialect it means "noisy waters."

Even as Spain was busy negotiating with the United States to solidify its holdings in the Southwest, Mexicans were preparing to sever Mexico's ties with Spain. The Mexicans declared their independence in 1821, taking with them those sections of the Southwest formerly controlled by Spain: California, Nevada, Texas, Utah, Arizona, and New Mexico, as well as parts of Wyoming, Colorado, and the Oklahoma panhandle.

Trader William Becknell, who left Missouri in the summer of 1821 on an expedition for trading "Horses, Mules and catching Wild Animals of every description," proved a particular beneficiary of Mexican independence. Heading toward the Raton Pass in Colorado, he and his cohorts ran into Mexican soldiers, who informed them of the Southwest's new allegiance. Becknell's expedition became the first American party to arrive in Santa Fe after Mexico's independence. Becknell returned the next year with three wagons, in addition to a pack train and thirty men. The party crossed the Cimarron River west of Dodge City, Kansas, following it and the Canadian River through the mountains to San Miguel and on to Santa Fe. It was the first time wagons traversed what was to become the legendary Santa Fe Trail.

During the decade that followed, Americans were on the move throughout the Southwest. In Arizona, trappers traveled in search of furs. Peter S. Ogden, a trapper and explorer who was employed by the Hudson's Bay Company, discovered and followed the Humboldt River into Nevada in 1828–9. During a later exploration, he traveled from Oregon through the Great Basin to the Colorado River on his way to the Gulf of California. The fur trade provided an important economic incentive for exploration, although Ogden described its harsh life as one that "makes a man sixty in a few years."

Opposite: "Her Heart's Strength: On the Trail of Tears" (1990), by Cherokee painter Jeanne Walker Rorex, depicts the nineteenth-century journey made by displaced Native Americans from the Southeast to Indian Territory in what is now Oklahoma.

Below: The military post at Fort Davis, Texas, was established in 1854 to protect travelers on the Overland Trail. Spanish explorers first passed through in 1583; Anglo settlers did not arrive until the 1840s.

Above: This late nineteenth-century photograph shows a Mexican-American family shucking corn in New Mexico. Corn, or maize, had been a staple of the Southwest diet for thousands of years.

Capitalizing on the newly opened trade route to New Mexico, fur trader Charles Bent and his brother William set off in 1829 on the Santa Fe Trail, using oxen to carry their goods. At the Cimarron cutoff, they were attacked by several hundred Kiowa braves, but the caravan made it to Santa Fe. In 1830 Bent joined Ceran St. Vrain to form Bent, St. Vrain and Company, eventually the largest mercantile business in the Southwest. Building Bent's Fort in Colorado in 1833, Bent and St. Vrain traded Mexican blankets and buffalo robes from the Plains country.

Trade stimulated the opening of other parts of the Southwest. Mexican trader Antonio Armijo was the first person known to reach Los Angeles from Santa Fe. Armijo and his party spent the winter of 1829–30 traveling over the Old Spanish Trail, which went from Santa Fe through southwest Colorado and Utah to California. Fur trader William Wolfskill, who was among those who had traveled with Becknell over the Santa Fe Trail in 1822, formed his own caravan in 1830 and also traveled over the Old Spanish Trail. This was the first time the route was used successfully for pack trains, and this trek initiated a lively trade between New Mexico and California.

Joseph Reddeford Walker entered the Santa Fe trade in 1820. Joining Benjamin Bonneville's 1832 expedition as a guide and trapper, he led Bonneville's 1833–4 excursion from Green River, Utah, to California, following the Humboldt River's course through Nevada and the Humboldt Sink. His expedition may have been the first to see Yosemite Valley. The Humboldt-Salt Lake route was later used by gold rushers heading for California.

Texas's story had taken a twist of its own. In 1821 the first American settlers came from the east and north into what was now the newly independent Mexico's state of Texas. A Connecticut Yankee who had lost his fortune in Missouri, Moses Austin had received a grant of 200,000 acres of Texas land when it still belonged to Spain. He died before he could take possession of it, and his son Stephen took over. Stephen Austin planned a colony for the lower Colorado and Brazos Rivers, north of present-day Austin. When the Mexicans refused at first to honor Austin's agreement with the Spanish, he went to Mexico City to negotiate. The result was the new Empresario system, in which agents like Austin were granted free land in exchange for agreeing to set up a legal system, create land records, arrange trade with the United States, encourage infrastructure construction, and attract settlers to their lands.

Three hundred families, later called the "Old Three Hundred," founded the first Texas settlements at Washington-on-the-Brazos and Columbus and farmed cotton there. In 1823 Austin established San Felipe de Austin to serve as the colonial capital of Texas. As American settlers poured into Texas, they set up their own communities, quickly outnumbering Hispanic settlers. Most refused to become Mexican citizens, convert to Roman Catholicism, or learn Spanish, all of which had been conditions accepted by Austin.

The instability of the fledgling Mexican government meant frequent changes to the Empresario system, but Austin managed to remain abreast of them. When Mexico passed a law that ended immigration in 1830, Austin found a loophole and continued to bring in settlers. Feeling ran high for creating an independent Texas. In 1829 President Andrew Jackson had offered to buy Texas from Mexico, but the offer was refused.

Below: The Fall of the Alamo, *shown here in a painting by Theodore Gentile, occurred in 1836, when 145 Texas rebels were killed by Mexican General Santa Anna's force of 6,000. Texas was still a Mexican province at the time.*

Above: *Survivors of the victorious Texas force at the Battle of San Jacinto (1836) pose for a portrait. Sam Houston led the Texan fighters, who defeated Mexican General Santa Anna.*

When General Antonio López de Santa Anna became the president of Mexico in 1833, he proved to be an erratic, sometimes absent, leader, and other politicians blocked his reforms. However, the move to encourage settlement in the Mexican states of the Southwest was further promoted in 1833 by passage of the Secularization Act, which provided for lay settlement of what had been considered mission country. But by this time, even many residents of Mexican and Spanish descent in Texas were becoming dissatisfied with taking orders from the government in Mexico City. Things only got worse in 1834, when Santa Anna made himself the virtual dictator of Mexico, abolishing the federal constitution and taking personal control of each Mexican state.

In 1833 a group comprising mainly American settlers had held a convention at San Felipe de Austin and drafted a petition for independence that Austin took to Mexico City. Mexican president Santa Anna agreed to repeal the 1830 anti-immigration law, but he refused to grant Texas independence.

Because he had presented the petition, Austin served time in a Mexican jail in 1834–5 for insurrection.

Released in July 1835, Stephen Austin was perhaps one of the last to give up on the dream of an Anglo-American state of Texas as part of Mexico. By now, Americans in Texas wanted no part of such an arrangement, and on October 1, in Gonzales, Texas, a group of them declared war on Mexico. At first the Texan rebels claimed they merely wanted to see Mexico's 1824 constitution reinstated. Then, with Austin in charge of their troops, they defeated Mexican soldiers at San Antonio and took control of the town. In November, Austin went to Washington as a commissioner whose responsibility was to negotiate recognition for a new Republic of Texas.

In response to the unruly Texans who had taken over San Antonio in 1835, Santa Anna brought in his army. The Americans holed up in the legendary fortified former mission called the Alamo. Refusing to surrender from February 23 to March 6, 1836, despite the fact that they were outnumbered by a factor of thirty to one, some 190 Americans fought to the death. Among the frontiersmen who lost their lives here were Davy Crockett, Jim Bowie, and William B. Travis. Estimates of Mexican casualties range from 1,200 to 1,600.

Meanwhile, in Washington-on-the-Brazos, another group of Americans met on March 1 and declared Texas independent. Politician and plantation owner David G. Burnet was named the president, and former Tennessee governor Sam (Samuel) Houston, the commander-in-chief of their army. Later that month, slave trader James W. Fannin and some 300 Americans were captured and executed by the Mexicans at Goliad, Texas, which was a strategic point for Gulf Coast supply routes.

Led by Houston, on April 21, 1836, the outraged Americans retaliated by defeating Santa Anna's army at San Jacinto with "Remember the Alamo!" as their battle cry. Their victory foreshadowed the conclusion of 300 years of Hispanic rule over the Southwest. Houston was elected president of the Texas Republic that fall and went to Washington to appeal for annexation. At first Congress refused, calling the Texas rebellion a "slaveocracy conspiracy," but recognition of the republic by President Andrew Jackson came in 1837. Texas was finally annexed as the twenty-eighth state on December 29, 1845, by President James K. Polk, thus provoking a more violent and decisive conflict with Mexico.

Left: *Detail from Mission San Jose y San Miguel de Aguayo in San Antonio, Texas. Called the "Queen of the Missions," it was founded in 1720.*

Below: *The Alamo, as it appears today, is actually a complex of buildings called Mission San Antonio de Valero and Mission San Antonio de Bexar. Construction of the church shown here, the building most typically associated with the Alamo, began in 1744.*

An organization that emerged in 1826 and still exists today—the Texas Rangers—commissioned as state law enforcement officers and headquartered in Austin, became the defenders of the new republic. They provided important protection to settlers from both Mexican and Native American marauders from 1836 to 1845.

Unrest bedeviled the Mexicans in other parts of their North American territories: independence was an issue in California as well as in Texas. Juan Bautista Alvarado, who became governor in 1834, declared the state's independence from Mexico in 1836. The Mexican government simply ignored Alvarado's claim, and he was removed as governor in 1842.

Meanwhile, in Santa Fe, the New Mexico governor, Albino Perez, was assassinated when civil combat erupted there in 1837. The dispute involved Mexicans, Native Americans, and others who objected to high taxes. The insurgents captured Santa Fe's Palace of the Governors but were defeated at La Canada by Manuel Armijo, who then took over administration of the state for the Mexican government.

When a band of Texan soldiers and merchants marched into eastern New Mexico in 1841 with plans for annexation, Armijo arrested them. They were sent to Mexico but later released. Hostilities continued in 1842, when Mexican soldiers invaded Texas and captured San Antonio. An 1843 truce proved merely a temporary respite as war clouds gathered ominously.

In 1842 a young army officer, John Charles Frémont, was requested by the U.S. topographical bureau to survey the Platte and Kansas Rivers. This was the first of four major expeditions (1842–8) during which he explored much of the American West. Having met Kit (Christopher) Carson in 1842, he used him as a guide on this and his next two expeditions. With help from his wife, the writer Jessie Ann Benton Frémont, Frémont drafted official reports, the first of which included a map that "changed the entire picture of the West and made a lasting contribution to cartography." Particularly significant was his new depiction of Nevada and its Great Basin, independent of drainage outside its own system of lakes, rivers, and creeks.

Refusing to recognize an independent Texas or to accept the Rio Grande as an international boundary, Mexico broke off diplomatic relations with the United States in 1845. Under orders from President Polk, General Zachary Taylor moved his troops from Louisiana to Texas and eventually to the Rio Grande near Corpus Christi, where he established a camp he called Fort Texas. He ordered the U.S. Navy to blockade the Rio Grande at its mouth. On April 25, 1846, Mexican troops crossed the river and attacked a small American patrol, killing eleven. Taylor won the next two skirmishes at the Palo Alto Plain and at Resaca de Palma, Texas, May 8 and 9. Congress declared war on Mexico on May 12 and authorized Polk to call up 50,000 volunteers. On May 18, Taylor crossed the Rio Grande into Mexico and captured the northern Mexican city of Matamoros. The United States was now engaged in a full-scale war with its own neighbour, Mexico.

The formation of a Texas Republic encouraged American settlers within California to try for a republic there. With the U.S. government applying diplomatic pressure for annexation, tensions were high between the Americans and Mexican authorities. By April of 1846, Frémont had crossed into northern California, ostensibly on another map-making expedition; in fact, he had secret instructions to assist Californians in any efforts to join the Union. By that May he was bivouacked near Sutter's Fort, the base of the land holdings of Swiss immigrant and entrepreneur John Sutter. Realizing that the Americans were ready to rebel, Frémont resigned his army commission in order to join the civilian uprising himself.

On June 10, a group of the rebels encouraged by Frémont seized the town of Sonoma and arrested the retired Mexican general Mariano Vallejo. En route, they rode behind a crude home-made flag, emblazoned with a single red star and a grizzly bear. Then, in Sonoma, they declared California an independent republic and displayed their "nation's" new flag. (This design would eventually become part of California's state flag.) Frémont took charge and journeyed south to occupy an empty fort at San Francisco. On July 9, the Bear Flag Republic came to

Left: *Bear Flag Monument in Sonoma Plaza commemorates the raising of the flag in 1846 to signify California's freedom from Mexico. It was made from manta cloth and a lady's petticoat.*

Overleaf: *Taos Pueblo in northern New Mexico is the oldest continuously inhabited site in the United States, established long before 1540, when Coronado arrived. It is the most northern of Rio Grande pueblos, and its inhabitants are believed to be descendants of either the prehistoric Chaco or Anasazi people.*

an end when U.S. Navy lieutenant Joseph Warren Revere (a grandson of Paul Revere) replaced the Bear Flag flying at Sonoma with the American national flag. That same day, naval captain John Montgomery landed at San Francisco and claimed it for the United States.

During the next few months, the American forces in California came under the direction of U.S. Navy commodore Robert Stockton, and most of the fighting was centered around both Los Angeles and San Diego. Stockton, with the support of Frémont's battalion, took Los Angeles in August and placed all of California under martial law. Frémont returned to northern California and Stockton left U.S. Marine lieutenant Archibald Gillespie in charge of southern California. On September 22, a group of Mexican-Californians, led by José Maria Flores, revolted, and by September 29 they had taken back Los Angeles, forcing Gillespie and his men to leave the area on a merchant ship. By December 1, though, both Stockton and Frémont were back in the Los Angeles area in an attempt to put down this revolt.

With a mixed lot of U.S. military and civilians engaged in the war in California, and Zachary Taylor fighting the Mexicans in northern Mexico, General Stephen Watts Kearny left Fort Leavenworth, Kansas, in June 1846, entered Santa Fe, and took control of New Mexico with the Army of the West. That September he set off for California with 300 men. Arriving in time to engage Mexican forces at San Pascual, north of San Diego, on December 6, 1846, the Americans suffered heavy casualties in the battle, but the Mexicans did not pursue their advantage.

While still in Santa Fe, Kearny had assigned several officers to lead other expeditions. He had ordered Captain Philip St. George Cooke to open a way to California by leading a band of some 400 Mormons, known as the Mormon Battalion. Driving southwest from Santa Fe into Sonora, Mexico, and then north and west through Arizona, Cooke and his men entered Tucson in December. They rejoined Kearny's own forces in California on January 29, 1847, when the Mexicans in southern California were no longer a threat. Stockton, with reinforcements from Kearny, defeated the Mexican army in a skirmish on the San Gabriel River outside Los Angeles on January 8, 1847. On January 10, the Americans retook Los Angeles and set up a government there shortly afterward.

Kearny had assigned another group of soldiers to Colonel Alexander Doniphan, and after leaving Santa Fe in November 1846, this band of some 856 men made an epic three-month march to Chihuahua, Mexico, capturing El Paso on their way. Meanwhile, Kearny left Colonel Sterling Price in command of U.S. troops in New Mexico, where pockets of resistance to American control remained. Charles Bent, the former fur trader, was now the American governor of New Mexico, and he had gone to visit family and friends in Taos; along with five other Americans, he was killed there by a group of Pueblo Indian and Mexican insurgents. Colonel Price chased the rebels to Taos Pueblo and, in February 1847, defeated them. The skirmish proved the greatest resistance to American control of New Mexico during the Mexican War.

Partly for political reasons, partly for strategic ones, President Polk put General Winfield Scott in command of the army that landed at Vera Cruz and moved across the heartland of Mexico. Then on September 14, 1847, Scott's forces captured Mexico City, and the war was over. It was February 2, 1848, however, before the Treaty of Guadalupe Hidalgo was signed. The vast expanse of the Southwest, reaching from Texas to the Pacific Ocean, now belonged to the United States. As it happened, just nine days before signature of the treaty, gold was discovered near the same Sutter's Fort where Frémont had helped to launch the rebellion against Mexico. The stage was set for a brand-new era in the history and fortunes of this fascinating region.

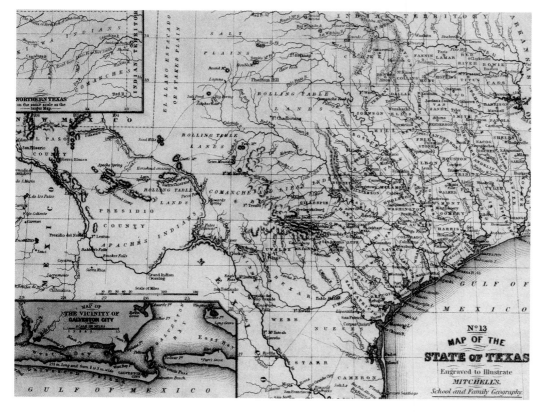

Left: This map of Texas after the U.S.-Mexican War was drawn by J.H. Young and was first published in Mitchell's School and Family Geography (*1858*).

Overleaf: El Capitan in Guadalupe National Park near Salt Flat, Texas, rises more than 8,000 feet from sea level. The Guadalupe Mountains provided the last stronghold in Texas for the Apache.

Struggling
Toward
Unity

Previous page:
The sun rises over the west Texas panhandle, where cattlemen and sheepherders converged to find new grazing grounds in the nineteenth century, and Longhorn cattle replaced the buffalo.

Below: *A Mormon family poses in front of their log cabin near Snowflake, Arizona. Founded in 1878, Snowflake was named after its founders, Apostle Erastus Snow and Mormon land agent William Flake.*

The Treaty of Guadalupe Hidalgo in 1848 ended the Mexican-American War, and the United States became a continent-wide nation, while bumping Mexico from its status as the fourth-largest country in the world and fulfilling what an 1845 editorial called "our manifest destiny." The United States acquired California, Nevada, Utah, and most of Arizona, as well as sections of New Mexico, Colorado, and Wyoming: 530,000 square miles at a cost of $15 million.

New Mexico did not submit readily to U.S. military rule after the 1848 treaty. Two factions dominated New Mexico politics. James S. Calhoun and Manuel Alvarez headed one—the party had favored statehood—while Ceran St. Vrain and Thomas Cabeza de Baca led the party in favor of territorial status. Alvarez, Spanish-born and a Mexican citizen, had helped establish Brigadier

General Stephen Kearny's occupation of New Mexico during the Mexican-American War. After serving in the 1847 General Assembly, Alvarez held a variety of territorial offices. St. Vrain, who had been a partner in the Bent, St. Vrain Trading Company, lobbied for territorial status. Military rule continued until the region, which included most of Arizona and parts of Colorado, Utah, and Nevada, was granted territorial status in 1850, with Calhoun as its first governor.

By 1849 the entire nation seemed to be looking West, but few chose to settle in the arid, mountainous, and still dangerous Southwest. All too often, Comanche and Kiowa braves still attacked wagon trains along the Sante Fe Trail. One of the few people who did choose to settle in the region during this period was Brigham Young, the leader of the Mormon Church. Persecution

Left*: An illustration from* Harper's Weekly, *March 1870, portrays an Indian attack on a wagon train traveling the Oregon/California Trail. In fact, such attacks were relatively rare.*

had pushed the Mormons out of Missouri and Illinois. In 1847 Young and 147 fellow members of the Church of Jesus Christ of Latter-Day Saints moved into the Great Salt Lake Valley in present-day Utah. The Salt Lake Valley, Young announced, "is a good place to make Saints and it is a good place for Saints to live. It is the place the Lord has appointed and we shall stay here until He tells us to go somewhere else."

Surviving a rough winter by living on roots, thistles, and ox-hide soup, the Mormons, under Young's leadership, petitioned Congress to establish a new state in the Salt Lake Valley region. It was to be called Deseret, after The Book of Mormon's designation for the honey bee, symbol of co-operation and support. Deseret was to include Utah and Nevada, as well as sections of Wyoming, Colorado, and California. However, politicians in Washington didn't see things the way Young and his followers did. They partially granted the Mormons' ambitious request, but reduced its size by three-quarters, designating the region a territory and

naming it Utah after the Ute tribe. In 1850 President Millard Fillmore appointed Young superintendent of Indian affairs and governor of the new territory.

In present-day Nevada, Mormons Captain Joseph DeMont and Hampton S. Beatie arrived from Salt Lake City in 1850 to establish that state's first trading post. Nevada's first permanent settlement, it was initially known as Mormon Station, then renamed Genoa in 1856. It served as the Carson County seat in the Utah territory until 1861. Nevada remained part of the Utah territory, although more in name than in fact. Utah territory and federal agents each formed vigilante groups and set up a series of temporary governments in 1851, 1857, and 1859. In 1859 planning progressed as far as a constitutional convention, with Isaac Roop elected as the first governor of a provisional territory separate from Utah. Nevada finally achieved territorial status in 1861, not long after the Confederacy was first formed, and President Abraham Lincoln appointed James W. Nye as governor.

Below: Bodie, California, is a mining ghost town managed as a State Historic Park site since 1962. It dates back to 1859, when William S. Bodie discovered gold near what is now called Bodie Bluff.

Just before the Mexican-American peace treaty was signed in January 1848, James Marshall discovered gold while building a lumber mill for the Swiss entrepreneur John Augustus Sutter, near Sacramento, California. Within six months, the streets of San Francisco virtually emptied. Men left in droves to prospect on the American River, the Feather River, the Trinity River, tributaries of the Sacramento River, and in the foothills of the Sierra Nevada. Native Americans were hired, sometimes virtually enslaved, to pan for gold.

Word of Marshall's discovery spread quickly and "gold fever" struck hard across the nation. Americans with dreams of making their fortune prospecting for gold were soon streaming across the West en route to California. Horses, oxen, even camels, were used for the trek to gold country, but mules proved to withstand the climate and the rigors of the trip best. Some came by sea, either traveling all the way around Cape Horn, or breaking the sea voyage to slog across the Isthmus of Panama. William Swain, one new prospector who left Youngstown, New York, by steamer in April 1849, wrote: "The boat shoots along like an arrow, and as she leaves far in the distance objects familiar to me…I feel that she bears me to my destiny." Others flocked in from South America, France, England, Germany, and Italy.

Left: *Keane Wonder Mine, now in ruins, acquired its name when an out-of-work Irish miner named Jack Keane discovered gold at this site in Death Valley, California. One of the hiking trails in Death Valley National Park passes this historic ruin.*

In little more than twelve months, California's population ballooned to 90,000, and a lobby for statehood soon formed. A convention to formulate a state-constitution proposal was held in Monterey. The proposal prohibited slavery, not so much because of enlightened views, but out of fear that slaves might be involved in gold prospecting. While African Americans would not be allowed to vote, married women could own property—a first in the nation. California's bid for statehood caused problems for Congress, where the issue of the extension of slavery was being hotly debated. After much wheeling and dealing, the Compromise of 1850 made California the fifty-first state. The normal waiting period for statehood was waived for California, but in other parts of the Southwest—specifically the new territories of Utah and New Mexico—slavery was entirely unrestricted. However, California's new citizens had nothing to boast of when it came to their treatment of the region's Native Americans, who had always lived in relatively small, dispersed, and independent groups. The incoming settlers simply set about to take their lands and kill them off, and of those who were not killed outright, many died from disease or starvation.

When the United States made the Gadsden Purchase in 1853, the strip of land between Texas and California became the last territorial addition on the continent, with the exception of Alaska. It encompassed more than 29 million acres of New Mexico and Arizona, and was bought from a financially distressed Mexico by the U.S. minister to Mexico, James Gadsden. The purchase helped establish a natural boundary line between the United States and its neighbor to the south. It was also intended to enable construction of a rail line from the Mississippi River to the Pacific Ocean. With the politics of abolition and the approaching Civil War raging around the $10-million purchase, the railway was, however, never built.

of War, adding another layer of complication to the handling of Indian-Anglo affairs. Conflicts varied from territory to territory, but all resulted in much the same fate for the natives.

Long before the arrival of Anglo-Americans, the Ute tribe had made its home in western Colorado and eastern Utah. For the most part, Mormon settlers lived peaceably with the tribe, although Mormons killed 27 Utes in a dispute over livestock theft in 1849 and drove the others away from their settlements. By 1850 the Bureau of Indian Affairs was planning tribal territories where Indians might learn agriculture skills and be converted to Christianity. Colonel William Selby Harney, who had already earned the nickname "Squaw Killer," was dispatched in 1855 to establish order in Utah and Kansas. He proved as punitive to Utah's Mormons as he had been earlier toward Native Americans. Planning to hang Brigham Young and other church elders, Col. Harney was transferred to Oregon before he could carry out the executions. It would be 1867 before the Indian wars in Utah territory came to end.

When mining in the Colorado Rockies generated a new influx of settlers during the 1860s, serious friction began to develop between the newcomers and Native Americans. After a giant vein of silver ore was discovered in Virginia City, Nevada, in 1859, it quickly became the richest mining city in the Old West. Prospector Henry Comstock claimed credit for the discovery, although others had actually made it. More than 6,000 miners lived in Nevada's mining camps by 1860, and the government went to war that year with the Paiute in Nevada. In western Colorado, Ute chief

Above: Nai-chi-ti, also known as Nachez, poses with his wife. The son of Cochise, he succeeded his brother Taza as chief of the Chiricahua, who came from Arizona and were the most feared of the Apache tribes. He is buried in the Apache Cemetery at Fort Sill Military Reservation in Oklahoma.

From early on, the U.S. government had attempted to follow a policy of maintaining peaceful relations with the Native Americans who inhabited the Southwest. To this day, the Southwest remains home to the most Native Americans and has the most native-controlled property in the nation. Enforcement of laws regulating tribes was delegated to the territorial governors. As more and more Anglos moved into the Southwest, however, disputes occurred with increasing frequency. Each new territory acquired military posts and protection from native attacks. When the Department of the Interior was created in 1849, responsibility for relations with the Native American tribes was transferred to it from the Department

Ouray negotiated a treaty for 16 million acres in 1863 to establish a permanent reservation for his people.

Among the most prominent of the Native Americans who inhabited Arizona and New Mexico were the Apache. Although they had a reputation as nomadic marauders, in fact, they derived a quarter of their livelihood from agriculture. Acquiring Spanish horses, they had become expert equestrians by the end of the seventeenth century. An incident in February 1861 had already initiated a series of conflicts called the Apache Wars that lasted for twenty years. The wars began when Lieutenant George N. Bascom, from Fort Buchanan, Arizona, accused Chiricahua Apache chief Cochise of stealing cattle and kidnapping a child. Cochise claimed he had not been involved and met with Lt. Bascom at Apache Pass in the Chiricahua Mountains of southeast Arizona to negotiate. Violating a truce agreement, Bascom held the chief captive, but Cochise escaped by slitting the tent where he was confined. Bascom hanged Cochise's brother and two nephews, who had not escaped. Cochise retaliated by taking three Americans captive and murdering them when Bascom refused to release Cochise's people. Within two months, approximately 150 settlers died.

The U.S. military confronted nearly 30,000 Apache with 3,000 soldiers, a ten-to-one ratio. On July 15, 1862, it took howitzers with 12-pound shells to rout Chiefs Mangas Coloradas and Cochise, with 500 warriors, from the water hole at Apache Pass, which the Indians had sealed off. As a result of the battle, which led to the first Medal of Honor award, Fort Bowie was built to protect Apache Pass.

Once the Civil War broke out, efforts to subdue the Southwest's native population grew even stronger. In New Mexico, the government decided to relocate the Navajo, after recurring problems with both raids and sheep rustling. In 1861 Colonel Edward R.S. Canby, New Mexico's army commander, wrote: "There is now no choice between their absolute extermination or their removal and colonization at points so remote from the settlements as to isolate them entirely from the inhabitants of the territory." The assumption had already been made that New Mexico belonged to the settlers. The First New Mexico Volunteers, led by Kit Carson, fought the

Below: Goyathlay, better known to Anglo-Americans as Geronimo, was a Bedonkohe Apache born in 1829 in New Mexico. As leader of the last group of American Indians who formally surrendered to the United States, he is the most famous of the Apache. His name means "one who yawns."

Below: These wagon wheels are located in the ghost town Rhyolite, which became the third-largest city in Nevada by 1908. Named for a volcanic rock that is variegated in color, Rhyolite was called the Queen City of Death Valley and lies four miles west of Beatty, Nevada.

Mescalero Apaches and the Navajo from 1862 to 1864, when they succeeded in confining these tribes to reservations on the Pecos River at Bosque Redondo. A proud and fierce people, the Apache continued to raid Anglo settlements until the surrender of their chief Goyathlay, known as Geronimo, in 1886. In the course of the Apache Wars, thousands of whites were mutilated and murdered, and an equal number of Indians were scalped, poisoned, and shot.

Most of the Southwest sided with the Confederacy during the War Between the States. The exceptions were California and Nevada. No Civil War battles were fought in California, and the state had its own Union Army Department. In 1862 a California volunteer force under the leadership of General James H. Carleton marched from southern California to join General Edward R.S. Canby's troops in New Mexico. Canby had already defeated Confederate general Henry Hopkins Sibley, and Carleton's arrival caused Sibley's Confederate forces to retreat into Texas.

Lincoln's speedy proclamation of statehood for Nevada was no doubt influenced by the territory's leanings toward the Union's cause. The state played a significant role during the great conflict because of its silver and other mineral resources, which were coveted by both North and South.

Many of Arizona's settlers came from Confederate states, and Arizona sent a delegate to the Confederate Congress, although popular opinion favored the Union. Between June and August 1861, Colonel John Baylor of Texas occupied southwestern New Mexico and Arizona and proclaimed the territories part of the Confederacy. Confederate troops from Texas occupied Santa Fe and Albuquerque, as well as much of the rest of the territory. With the Southwest in danger of domination by the Confederacy, General Edward Canby led Union troops, primarily volunteers from Colorado, in two battles in March 1862, one near Santa Fe at Glorieta Pass and the other at Apache Canyon, recapturing New Mexico for the Union. In 1863 the Federal Congress separated Arizona from New Mexico and created the Arizona territory; its new governor took up residence in a log cabin in Fort Whipple, which was eventually called Prescott.

Left: *Mojave village life on the Colorado River is portrayed in this engraving made for the 1855 railway survey from the Mississippi to the Pacific by the U.S. War Department. The Mojave Reservation today covers parts of Nevada and Arizona. This tribe was called the "People by the River."*

At the time of the Civil War, Oklahoma, called Indian Territory, remained under Native American control, and many Oklahoma Indians were slave-owners. The Confederate loyalist Albert Pike persuaded some of the tribes to form an alliance in anticipation of their joining the Confederacy. John Ross, the foremost Cherokee leader of the nineteenth century, tried to remain neutral, but when the Confederate forces won a battle at Wilson's Creek, Missouri, he was forced to pledge Cherokee support for the Confederacy. One Cherokee warrior, Stand Watie, became a brigadier general in the Confederate army. Nevertheless, some of Oklahoma's natives did fight on the Union side.

Texas stood firmly aligned with the Confederacy, seceding from the Union before Lincoln's inauguration: federal posts and property surrendered to the Confederates on January 18, 1861. But after Union army victories on the Mississippi, at Vicksburg and Port Hudson, Union troops returned to Texas and won an engagement at Brownsville in 1863. Battles ensued at Galveston, the Sabine Pass, Corpus Christi, Fort Esperanza, and near the mouth of the Rio Grande. The major Texas engagement was called the Red River Campaign, fought from March through May 1864. On May 13, 1865, the last major battle of the Civil War was fought at Palmito Hill, Texas, on the Rio Grande River, with Texas Rangers filling out the Confederate ranks. Their victory, of course, had no effect on the outcome of the war, which had ended that April.

In the years after the Civil War, lawlessness was common in Texas, and the Lone Star State did not fare at all well in economic terms during the Reconstruction era. Ninth among the states in per capita wealth in 1869, by 1880 it was just thirty-sixth. In 1867 Congress's Radical Republicans succeeded in denying Texas readmission to the Union and declared military rule there. A convention of radical elements in Texas drafted a new constitution in 1869, leading to readmission the following year. Texas politics were dominated by the Ku Klux Klan and carpetbag-scalawag Republicans until 1874, when

Above: Geronimo's final surrender in September 1886, at Skeleton Canyon in Arizona, is depicted in an engraving from Harper's Weekly, *October 1886. Geronimo epitomized the Apache values of courage and aggressiveness in combat.*

Richard Coke was inaugurated governor. In 1876 Coke initiated the writing of a new constitution, which limited government power, and a succession of former Confederate sympathizers won election to office for the next thirty years.

As tension between Anglos and Native Americans continued, the U.S. Army took over at forts across the Southwest after the Civil War. In Colorado, the Cheyenne and Arapaho waged war against settlers in 1864, until a treaty was signed the following year. Plains Indians, however, did not always see why they should adhere to treaties signed by their chiefs. Between 1865 and 1891, the army fought twelve major battles with Indians. Major General Philip H. Sheridan planned a campaign that would catch Cheyenne, Arapaho, Kiowa, and Comanche warriors by surprise in their winter camps. U.S. troops left from Fort Bascom in New Mexico, Fort Lyon in Colorado, and Camp Supply in Indian Territory. At the

Washita River in western Oklahoma on November 27, 1868, Lieutenant Colonel George Armstrong Custer caught the Cheyenne as they slept and killed at least 100 in the attack, but he was forced to retreat when Arapaho warriors appeared on the scene.

Railroads, which began to spread like wildfire across the Midwest in the 1840s, reached California in 1869, creating the first transcontinental link to the East. The flood of settlers into California and the Southwest continued, but an economic downturn in the 1870s led to high unemployment rates there. The scapegoats for job-hungry malcontents were Chinese laborers. Hostility toward the Chinese started as early as 1849, when that ethnic group joined the original gold rush. In 1871 a Los Angeles mob killed at least eighteen Chinese in retaliation for the purported shooting of a Californian. By the 1876 national elections, "The Chinese Must Go" slogans fomented more riots, and abuse of

Chinese immigrants continued through the last decades of the nineteenth century, particularly in California. After the hard times of the 1870s, greater prosperity brought more immigrants to the state. Agriculture and industry flourished, and a land boom in southern California boosted the population.

Post-Civil-War Oklahoma saw the completion of the Missouri, Kansas and Texas Railroad from Kansas south to Sherman, Texas, in 1872. It was followed by The Atlantic and Pacific, which was later called the St. Louis and San Francisco. The Achison, Topeka and Santa Fe line was added in 1887, extending from Kansas to Fort Worth, Texas, and beyond.

In postwar New Mexico and Arizona, Apaches went back on the warpath after Tucson vigilantes murdered nearly 100 men, women, and children as they slept in the Camp Grant Massacre of 1871. In 1872 and 1873, Colonel George Crook fought Apache warriors in the Tonto Basin and at Salt River Canyon and Turret Butte. As a result, the Apache were confined to reservations. Led by Geronimo, they continued to resist until 1886, when General Nelson A. Miles eventually subdued them and Geronimo surrendered, although he did not understand the implications of his "unconditional" surrender. The legendary chief was sent to prison in Florida, where he remained for five years. Then he was transferred to Fort Sill, Oklahoma. Employed by the federal government as a scout, he remained there until his death.

Texas, Oklahoma, New Mexico, Colorado, and Kansas were the scene of further anti-Indian military operations in 1874 and 1875. In the Texas panhandle and western Oklahoma, Colonel Ranald Slidell MacKenzie forced Native Americans who had left their reservations to return there. In Arizona, Phoenix, which had been developed to supply Fort McDowell, became the new capital. In 1891 the Phoenix government offered a

Below: The Southern and Pacific Railroad lines met at Lathrop, California, as depicted here in 1878. The Western railroads were built primarily with Chinese labor and provided an important conduit for Wells Fargo shipments.

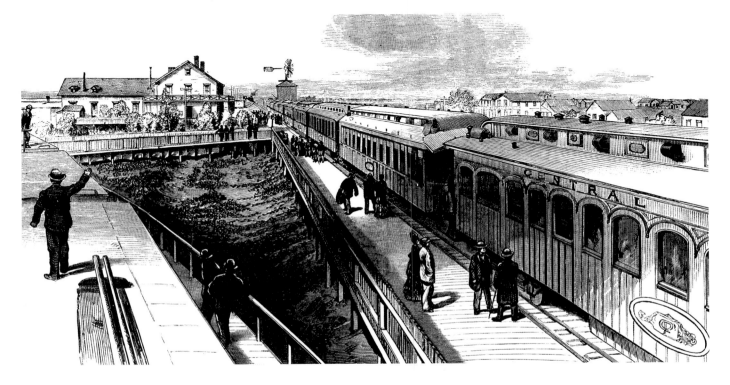

Above: *The OK Corral in Tombstone, Arizona, was the site of a legendary gunfight in 1881 involving Wyatt Earp, his brothers Morgan and Virgil, and their friend Doc Holliday. Their opponents were Ike Clanton, a cowboy who had inspired Holliday's wrath in a saloon the night before, Ike's brother Billy, and their two friends Frank and Tom McLaury.*

County War of 1878. Bonney was implicated in a string of murders from the time of the Lincoln County War and his 1879 arrest until his death at the hands of Lincoln County Sheriff Pat Garrett in 1880, at Stinking Springs, near Fort Sumter. As soon as General Lew Wallace was appointed governor of New Mexico, he declared amnesty between the principals of the Lincoln County War, but it was still necessary to establish martial law and use troops to put an end to the killing.

Oklahoma Native Americans paid a high price for their support of the Confederacy, with incoming settlers encroaching steadily on their territory. Texas ranchers drove their cattle herds through Oklahoma on the way to Kansas City rail terminals. Cattle owners leased millions of acres of open land, sometimes paying, sometimes not. In 1885 a federal law was passed enabling purchase of unused native lands by whites. The Dawes Severalty Act of 1887 devised a complicated system of dividing up Indian land still further. In 1889 President Benjamin Harrison opened unoccupied Oklahoma lands. Settlers then flooded in, causing Guthrie, which served as the first capital, and Oklahoma City to spring up practically overnight.

After the government bought all Indian claims to a tract of 2 million acres that was known as the Oklahoma District, an estimated 50,000 to 100,000 Kansas "Boomers" charged in at the sound of a bugle and staked their claims. It was April 22, 1889, and the Boomers proved to be outwitted by the "Sooners," as settlers who sneaked in illegally the night before were called. A year later, Oklahoma, including the Panhandle, which had been called No Man's Land, became a territory. In 1891 President Harrison opened even more

reward of $200 for every dead Indian, after the federal government closed a number of nearby forts. In spite of such abuses of Native Americans, the U.S. Congress authorized enlistment of 2,000 Indians as soldiers rather than scouts. However, the Indian enlistment program did not prove to be very successful.

The military containment of Native Americans was further complicated in New Mexico by disputes between cattlemen and merchants. In 1875 the Colfax County War pitted land speculators against politicians known as the Santa Fe Ring. The legendary Billy the Kid (William Bonney) was one of those involved in the fighting during the Lincoln

large tracts of land to settlers. During that period of the Southwest's history, present-day Oklahoma actually consisted of two territories: Oklahoma and Indian. For the Cherokee nation, it was the end of an era. They performed their last ritual Ghost Dance in 1892, the day before still more of their lands were opened to settlement.

The Dawes and Jerome Commissions, formed in Congress to oversee the so-called Five Civilized Tribes of Native Americans, concluded negotiations that gave 160 acres to each native man, woman, and child in Oklahoma Territory. But the agreement led to the largest land run in history, when the six

Left: *Pioneer Memorial United Methodist Church in Independence, California, dates back to 1871. Starting with the discovery of gold in 1848, California's population grew by leaps and bounds, and churches were established to serve the new residents.*

million acres of the Cherokee Outlet were opened to settlers. Similar land lotteries continued until 1905.

Despite the conflict and violence that often stained the Southwest, the region also inspired many colorful legends of Western America. One such story was the shootout at the OK Corral in Tombstone, Arizona, involving Wyatt Earp and his brothers Virgil and Morgan, along with their friend Doc Holliday, on October 25, 1881. Another

Right: *U.S. Army families enjoy a May Day picnic near Fort McDowell, Arizona, in 1875. The search for gold and other marketable ores had led to settlement of the area and construction of Fort McDowell in 1865, resulting in the forcible resettlement of the indigenous Yavapai tribe.*

chapter in the colorful history of the Southwest involved the $100,000 robbery by the Hughes Gang of the Texas and Pacific Railroad in 1895. The heist was one of the biggest of the era, but the bank robbers were captured a month later. There was also the Texas legend "Judge" Roy Bean, a barkeeper and justice of the peace who called himself the "law west of the Pecos." Bean became celebrated for his heavy-handed legal decisions, and in 1896 he organized a boxing match that he called the heavyweight championship of the world. Since boxing was illegal in Texas, the fight was held on an island in the Rio Grande near his bar, "The Jersey Lily."

Drawn by its geographical beauty and native culture, a number of artists found their way to Taos and Santa Fe, New

Mexico, just before the turn of the new century. Joseph Henry Sharp arrived first, in 1883, and returned ten years later to settle in Taos permanently. Two of Taos's best-known artists were Ernest Blumenschein and Bert Geer Phillips. Trained at the *École des Beaux Arts* in Paris, Blumenschein arrived in Taos Pueblo in 1897 on assignment from McClure's Magazine. He liked the Southwest so much that he returned frequently and eventually settled down there to live among the Indians, whom he painted. Phillips, who had also learned about Taos from Sharp during a chance meeting in Paris, traveled to the artist's colony with Blumenschein and never left. These men laid the groundwork for the eventual emergence of this region as a mecca for artists and tourists.

Above: African-American homesteaders pose in front of their new house near Guthrie, Oklahoma Territory, in 1889. Guthrie was one of only two towns where homesteaders could file a land claim on April 22, 1889, the day of the Great Land Run in Oklahoma Territory. Many of the homesteaders were "buffalo soldiers"— African-Americans from the Ninth and Tenth Cavalry.

Nature signaled the end of the century for the Southwest by way of a devastating hurricane that leveled Galveston, Texas, in the nation's worst natural disaster. Yet after a period marked by strife and division, the region that looked toward the twentieth century had changed dramatically, from a Spanish, Mexican, and Native American-dominated, mainly rural society to one moving steadily toward a world of industry, agriculture, and private enterprise controlled largely by the newcomers from the East.

Right: *Point Bolivar Light in Galveston, Texas, was constructed in 1872 on the site of an earlier lighthouse. During the devastating hurricane that hit the area on September 8, 1900, 125 Galveston residents took refuge inside the lighthouse.*

THE
SOUTHWEST
AT WORK

Above: *A Hispanic family stands on its New Mexico farm in this photograph dating from the late nineteenth century. Native Americans were the first to cultivate this land, which has been farmed over the centuries by the Spanish, by Mexican-Americans, and Anglo-Americans.*

Previous page: *The mining town of Virginia City, Nevada, is the site of the Comstock Lode, one of the largest bodies of ore in the world. Gold was the first mineral discovered there, in 1859, but the area's blue-gray mud, laden with silver, proved even more valuable.*

If the Southwest was the scene of considerable conflict and violence during the nineteenth century, those decades were also the most formative years for the region's commercial and industrial development. When that century opened, the Southwestern economy was dominated by subsistence agriculture. Before long, fur trading, fishing, mining, ranching, transportation, and millwork emerged as important occupations for laborers, followed eventually by jobs associated with oil drilling and production.

The Southwest did not begin as a commercial supplier of agricultural products like wheat, tobacco, corn, or cotton. Most settlers were concerned primarily with providing for their families, and subsistence farming prevailed throughout the region.

While New York led all the states in agriculture from 1850 through 1870, Southwestern farming had begun to provide enough competition that many New Yorkers began moving west to grow cotton. Many farmers from the states of Maryland, Virginia, and North Carolina who experienced topsoil loss relocated to Arkansas and Texas. Wheat cultivation moved into the Southwest in the mid-nineteenth century, particularly in Oklahoma, where winter wheat became the chief crop. In the Great Plains states of Texas, Oklahoma, and eastern New Mexico, the development of dry farming allowed wheat crops to flourish. This technique employed deep and frequent plowing to conserve moisture in areas with less than 20 inches of rainfall per year. But for most regional farmers, it would be irrigation that made the difference.

Farmers in Salt River Valley, outside of Phoenix, Arizona, began bringing water to their fields in 1867 by rehabilitating irrigation canals built by the Hohokam hundreds of years earlier. The Grand Valley Canal was built in 1883 at the fork of the Gunnison and Colorado Rivers near Grand Junction, Colorado, to irrigate the state's western farms. By 1894 Congress passed the Carey Act, giving one million acres of public land each to ten of the West's most arid states, with the proviso that they convert it into usable acreage or offer it to settlers in quarter-sections of 160 acres. The California Development Company started planning for reclamation of what was originally called the Colorado Desert, or the Salton Sink, in southern California in 1896. A canal traveling northward through Mexico into what was then renamed the Imperial Valley of California began diverting the course of the Colorado River at the turn of the century.

While the Midwestern states may be known as the nation's cornbelt, corn had long been a mainstay crop for most Southwestern farmers—starting, of course, with the Native Americans of the region. It appealed because of its high protein content—it provides a higher yield per acre than most other plant foods—and its adaptability to different soils. Tobacco, one of the major, slave-supported cash crops of the South, moved west in the nineteenth century, as Southern soil was depleted. Cotton had not become a major crop until the invention of the cotton gin in 1793. In 1790 the estimate of cotton bales produced in the United States hovered around 3,000. By 1857 close to 5.4 million bales were harvested, a large proportion of them in the Southwestern region. Farmers in Arkansas and Texas were major cotton producers.

With cotton exports supplying the textile mills of England, cotton was the nation's chief trade product until the start of the twentieth century. A labor-intensive crop, it relied on slaves, which helps explain Texas's pro-Confederacy leanings. In the years after the Civil War, freed slaves became sharecroppers, and Texas began to compete with such Southern states as Mississippi and Louisiana to become the "king" of cotton producers. Later, when the boll weevil made its way up from Mexico into Texas in 1892, farmers there diversified, raising more beef and dairy cattle. But Texas was still responsible for over a quarter of U.S. cotton production in 1899.

Fishing in the Southwest provided an important source of food for Native Americans and later for the American settlers who supplanted them. Chinook, coho, chum, pink and red or sockeye salmon, as well as steelhead trout, populated the waters of southern California. Indian fisheries at Pyramid Lake in Nevada also caught the attention of settlers heading to California.

Overleaf: Cotton fields spread out below the Gila Mountains near Safford, Arizona. Cotton, along with wheat, tobacco, and corn, was among the first cash crops grown by nineteenth-century settlers of the Southwest.

Below: A woman pours well water into a simple irrigation system in Santa Fe. Some of the first Native Americans in the region used irrigation.

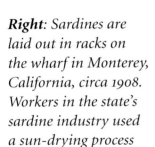

Right: Sardines are laid out in racks on the wharf in Monterey, California, circa 1908. Workers in the state's sardine industry used a sun-drying process to prepare the fish for shipping.

Dating back to colonial days, the trapping industry had been important to the developing Southwestern economy. European entrepreneurs dominated at first, and most American fur was exported to Europe. While the Old Northwest fur trade was controlled by the English and the Hudson's Bay Company, the Spanish relied on Panton, Leslie and Company, a Florida-based Scottish firm, in the easternmost parts of the Old Southwest where trapping was done. The most valuable fur was beaver, which was exported to Europe where it was much in demand for hats, coats, muffs, collars, cuffs, and linings.

Until the 1840s, when the beaver population began to decline from overtrapping, fur trading continued to spur both settlement and further exploration in the Southwest. The founding of the Missouri Fur Company in St. Louis in 1809 provided a shipping center for the region. Bound in 100-pound packs, the pelts traveled by river in birchbark canoes that carried as many as fourteen oarsmen, or in keelboats up to 60 feet long.

The "factory" system, dating back to the eighteenth century, had established a series of government posts, called factories, where natives could trade their furs for commercial goods. By the nineteenth century, however, the factory system was failing. Because these government-sponsored factories would not extend credit for Native American trappers to obtain traps, ammunition, and other necessities, the Indians often preferred to do business with independent traders, where the quality of the goods offered in exchange was usually better. With pressure from the American Fur Com-pany and St. Louis-based fur businesses, the government ended the factory system in 1822.

William H. Ashley was responsible for the procedure that replaced the factory system in the Southwest and elsewhere, known as the brigade-rendezvous system. Brigades of trappers were put under contract and salaried for specific time periods. Instead of traveling by boat, they were given packhorses. A rendezvous was held once a year, where the mountain-based trappers could trade their furs for goods from St. Louis. These events sometimes seemed more like carnivals than early trade conventions. They might feature wrestling, duels, horse races, shooting matches, fights, and buffalo chases. The rendezvous were also occasions for socializing with the native populations, and many trappers married Indian women. When Ashley sold his trade business in 1826 to a partnership that included explorer Jedediah Smith, the fur trade expanded into new areas of the Southwest. In the first overland expedition through the region, Smith traveled past the Great Salt Lake, over the Colorado Plateau, along the Colorado River to the Mojave Desert, and onward to California in search of new trapping grounds for exploitation.

Sheepherding—primarily the hardy Chaurro breed—originated in New Mexico when Mexican-born colonizer Juan de Oñate brought 1,000 rams and ewes with him in 1598. Basque immigrants, who had migrated to South America from the French-Spanish border region in Europe, moved into the Southwest to what were then Spanish provinces early in the nineteenth century. Their sheep and goat herds, along with cattle, were the economic mainstays of the many Spanish missions from San Francisco to San Antonio. Missionaries also taught regional Native Americans, the Navajo in particular, to tend sheep.

Below: Trappers pose with their burros, dogs, and pelts in Arizona Territory. Hunting and trapping provided important sources of income for Southwesterners in the nineteenth century.

Right: Barns of this style were built on Texas ranch land. Ranching provided sustenance for soldiers returning to Texas after the Civil War. Bluebonnets are in the foreground of this scene.

The Spanish had also introduced cattle into the Southwest. By the end of the eighteenth century, Spanish missions in Texas alone were estimated to have maintained cattle herds of close to 40,000 head. The Spanish also brought cattle herding to California, Arizona, and New Mexico. During the years of Spanish and Mexican control of California, cattle raising drove the economy, but its role diminished once that state joined the Union.

During the first quarter of the nineteenth century, cattle raising began to occupy increasing numbers of new settlers in Texas. By that time, cattle originally introduced by the Spanish were interbred with domestic cattle to produce a hardier strain of livestock that could tolerate the arid Great Plains. Four types prevailed: the Texas longhorn, the Spanish cow, the curly-haired or chino, and the mealy-nosed brown cow. Cattle raising as a major Southwestern industry traces it roots to the Mexican-American War, when Texas ranchers supplied the military with beef. Then, during the Civil War, Union blockades meant that cattle herds could not be driven east out of Texas, and longhorns ran wild, increasing to more than 5 million head by 1866.

Probably the most celebrated cattle ranch in the United States was started in 1853, when Richard King bought 75,000 acres from Juan Mendiola in Nueces County, Texas. King and his partner Mifflin Kennedy crossbred Brahman cattle and shorthorns to produce Santa Gertrudi, the first American beef-cattle breed. By the 1860s, King Ranch herds carried the world-famous Running W brand, and when King died in 1885, his wife took over, running the ranch until her death in 1925.

It was not until the post-Civil War era, however, that cattle ranching became a way of life across parts of the Southwest. Confederate soldiers returning home to Texas had no way to make a living except by rounding up wild cattle and selling them. Cattle empires cropped up in the Laredo, Corpus Christi, and San Antonio areas and spread throughout the region. Texas ranchers expanded onto

public land, particularly once the buffalo had been killed off and Native Americans confined to reservations. It took little more than a branding iron and a few cowboys to build a cattle barony by rounding up wild cattle and grazing them on "free air," as the grass and water of the public lands were called.

Herds had to be transported to central locations for sale and slaughter, so "the long drive," made famous by Western movies and actors like John Wayne, became the major means of transfer. The most famous of the routes used to herd cattle to market was the Chisholm Trail, which ran from San Antonio, Texas, to Abilene, Kansas. Named after Jesse Chisholm, it served as the major cattle highway from 1867 to 1871. But cattle herding did more than generate a commercial

industry for the country: although many of its essential tools and techniques came from Spanish Mexico, it created the cowboy culture that is so deeply embedded in American life. From blue jeans to cowboy hats and the Marlboro Man, cowboys set new standards for American dress, behavior, and recreation. The term rodeo, Spanish for "cattle ring," came to be used for cowboy competitions and exhibitions. Although the first rodeo was probably held in Pecos, Texas, on July 4, 1883, Prescott, Arizona, claims precedence as the town that awarded the first rodeo trophy, on July 4, 1888.

In the mid-nineteenth century, Santa Fe became an important commercial center. Its status was enhanced by the opening up of the Old Spanish Trail from Santa Fe through southern Utah and Nevada to San Diego and Los Angeles. Not all the traffic on the Old Spanish Trail was legitimate business. Horse thieves from southern California drove their animals east along the trail and slave traders, who had abducted Ute women and children for sale as domestics, used the route. Fur pelts and Missouri mules, bred out of Mexican donkeys and American mares, changed hands for clothing, household

Right: Cowgirls line up on their mounts at Millers 101 Ranch near Ponca City, Oklahoma. Founded in 1893, Millers 101 was a working ranch and from 1905 also home base for "Millers Wild West Show," which at the time was as celebrated as "Buffalo Bill's Wild West Show."

goods, guns, and clocks. Other Southwest trading centers of the era included Durango and El Paso del Norte, where European jewelry, mirrors, cologne, and champagne were popular items. It has been estimated that 363 wagons brought a million dollars' worth of foreign goods into the Southwest in 1846.

Commercial freighting companies used the Santa Fe Trail to carry military goods from Fort Leavenworth, Kansas, to Fort Union, New Mexico. By 1859 New Mexico had sixteen military posts, and everything from calico to pianos was shipped into the area. Alexander Majors,

who worked for the freighting firm of Russell, Majors and Waddell, became the king of the freighters, setting up strict rules for teamster conduct and treatment of animals on the mule trains.

California's gold rush, beginning in 1848, fueled travel on Southwestern commercial routes. Stagecoach baron George Giddings set up a mail route from San Antonio and Fort Davis to El Paso—then known as Franklin—and Santa Fe. John Butterfield's Overland Mail Company, created in 1858, ran 2,759 miles from St. Louis through Oklahoma to both Los Angeles and San Francisco in twenty-one days. Stagecoach travel was a lot more cramped and uncomfortable in the mid-nineteenth century than economy jet travel is today. Nine passengers would be packed onto three seats, two of which faced each other and necessitated alternating knees, with the outermost knee dangling unsupported outside, next to the wheel. The St. Louis–Tucson trip took sixteen days and nights, almost without stops except to change horses.

As thousands of would-be gold diggers flocked to California, new routes

Above: Texas longhorn cattle, as depicted here with several cowboys, were a mainstay of the nineteenth-century Texas economy. Hardy and aggressive, the longhorn breed evolved through natural selection and adaptation to the rugged Texas environment.

opened up in the Southwest. In 1849 a road was built from San Antonio to El Paso, giving access to Texas west of the Pecos River. Comanche and Kiowa raiding parties preyed on wagon trains heading for California, but Forts Davis and Stockton provided at least a modicum of protection. Fort Stanton protected travelers through southeastern New Mexico, while Fort Craig guarded the road between El Paso and Santa Fe. In the late 1850s, camels imported from the Near East were used as pack animals for U.S. Army surveying trips across Texas, Arizona, and New Mexico.

In addition to new freight, stagecoach, and express companies, the California gold rush boosted business for metal workers, lawyers, newspaper owners, politicians, saloonkeepers, gamblers, and prostitutes. New Southwestern cities developed to service gold-rush traffic, while others like Salt Lake City were forever changed. Agriculture and ranching flourished in response to the hordes of miners who needed to be fed.

Even Arizona, New Mexico, and Utah had their placer-gold deposits in alluvial sand and gravel. Swedish engineer and philanthropist Alfred Nobel, known today primarily for the prizes he inaugurated, helped the mining industry along through his invention of dynamite. It was first manufactured in San Francisco in

1866 using Nobel patents, and was soon used widely in mining and railroad construction. Along with such new devices, increasingly more complicated and expensive techniques would eventually convert mining from an individual enterprise into a full-scale industry.

Although he did not engage in mining, explorer and geologist John Wesley Powell turned himself into a legend in 1869 when he traversed 1,000 miles along the Green and Colorado Rivers, becoming the first non-native to pass, with nine others, through the Grand Canyon. On a second excursion in 1871, he mapped the Colorado Plateau for the federal government. His scientific work played a part in the formation of the U.S. Geological Survey in 1879, a federal organization whose mission still includes classification and examination of American mineral resources.

Silver, a less stable metal than gold, does not form placer deposits, combining instead with acids in run-off. It must be mined in its pure form from veins. The discovery of the Comstock Lode near Virginia City, Nevada, spurred a rush that lasted into the 1860s. It drew a second wind when four miners struck the "Big Bonanza" in 1873. The Comstock Lode was the first major U.S. gold-quartz ledge, and although predominately vein silver, it demanded new mining techniques. These included "square-set" timbering, the Cornish pump used to remove water from mines, and the Washoe Pan Process of amalgamation. The Sutro Tunnel, an invention of Adolph Sutro, burrowed four miles deep into Mount Davidson to tap into the Comstock Lode. Between 1859 and the early 1880s, an estimated $300 million, primarily in silver ore, was removed. Because so much silver was being taken from the Nevada mines, the federal government eliminated the silver dollar in 1873 and began to limit the amount of silver in its monetary system. Once that happened, the bottom fell out of the silver market. By the late 1870s, unemployed miners and members of associated industries were leaving the state in droves.

Gold and silver may be the glamour metals, but copper has played a far more important role in the nation's economic life. Arizona is home to four major copper deposits that date back to the Spanish occupation. Antonio de Espejo visited the Moqui in 1583, discovered copper, and began mining it. By the 1870s, copper sulfite mines went into full

Left: *Casa del Desierto was a Santa Fe railroad station and hotel complex in Barstow, California, that opened in 1911. It was considered one of the jewels of the Harvey House system, a series of dining rooms and boarding houses for Santa Fe Railroad passengers. It now houses the Mother Road Route 66 Museum and the Western America Railroad Museum.*

Above: "The Texas," built in 1855, was one of the first locomotive engines in the Lone Star State. It was used in the Great Locomotive Chase of the Civil War to pursue "The General," which had been hijacked by Union spies.

production at Clifton-Morenci, Globe, Bisbee, and Jerome, and copper out-produced gold and silver by the late 1880s. Mining companies like Phelps Dodge, W. A. Clark, and the Arizona Copper Company built towns and railroads and often controlled local politics.

Coal, the "poor relation" of the mining industry, was extracted in Oklahoma in the nineteenth century. Oklahoma's first coal mine began producing in 1872. New Mexico also had coal mines. Exposed to more dangers than other kinds of mining presented, coal miners worked in dark, sometimes very treacherous, underground shafts. Explosions were not unusual. An 1892 explosion in McAlester, Oklahoma, killed 100 coal miners and injured many others.

However, black gold, or petroleum, wins hands down as the most valuable mineral in the Southwest, far surpassing the worth of precious metals like gold and silver, as well as that of copper and coal. California led the region in oil exploration, which started there in the 1860s, although it would be 1892 before the first oil strike was made in the state. Kansas prospector Edward

Byrd drilled Oklahoma's first commercial oil well near Chelsea in 1889. Standard Oil Company subsidiary Forest Oil Company bought oil leases in Oklahoma Territory in 1895, and after they were transferred over to the Prairie Oil and Gas Company—another Standard subsidiary—Prairie connected the large Glenn pool in Oklahoma with Standard's East Coast refineries. The Red Folk-Tulsa oil field followed in 1901. That same year, discovery of oil and gas at Spindletop Field near Beaumont, Texas, revolutionized the state's economy as well as the petroleum industry.

The new communication industry, which dominates American commercial life today, had an early impact on the Southwest. It entered its infancy in the early 1850s, after Samuel F. B. Morse refined the earliest electromagnetic messaging system, the telegraph, in 1844. California became the first Southwestern state to acquire telegraph companies, with San Francisco and Los Angeles linked in 1860. Santa Fe almost gained a telegraph hook-up to Fort Smith, Arkansas, in 1858, when plans were developed to lay a cable at the bottom of the Canadian River, but it didn't materialize.

Congress stepped in on June 16, 1860, with the Pacific Telegraph Act, which offered a $40,000 subsidy to any company willing to build a telegraph line from the western boundary of Missouri through to San Francisco. The Overland Telegraph Company constructed lines from Carson City, Nevada, to Salt Lake City, using the Pony Express route. The Pacific Telegraph Company, a Western Union subsidiary, built a line from Omaha, Nebraska, to Fort Laramie, Wyoming. From there, the wires went through the South Pass to California.

Despite objections by Utah's Mormons, telegraph wires met in Salt Lake City on October 24, 1861, and the first message sent back East was to President Abraham Lincoln, assuring him of support for the Union. Gradually, all the cities of the Southwest were connected by telegraph, but not until after the turn of the century.

As the population tide swept into the region, homesteaders from the East clamored for the government to give them free land. They believed that their investment in developing unpopulated acreage was heavy enough without the additional burden of $1.25 per acre. Horace Greeley was one influential Easterner who rallied to their cause. When the Confederate states, who had different notions for development of the West, seceded, the way was cleared for passage of a land-grant act. President Abraham Lincoln signed the Homestead Act into law in 1862. It permitted any citizen to claim 160 acres of surveyed public land, gaining title after five years' residency.

Unfortunately, much of this land was grabbed by speculators and railroad builders. That same year, 1862, passage of the Morrill, or Land Grant, Act ensured that agricultural and engineering schools would be built in the Southwest, as well as the rest of the country. As more settlers moved into the Great Plains, larger tracts of land became necessary to make farming viable. The Timber Culture Act of 1873 allowed homesteaders to acquire 480 acres. It was followed in 1877 by the Desert Land Act, which offered 640 acres of desert land if the settler demonstrated that he could cultivate it through irrigation.

Railroads changed the face of the Southwest in the second half of the nineteenth century. The army conducted five transcontinental railroad surveys in the 1850s, two of which would have located the line through Texas, Arizona, and New Mexico. By 1862 Congress had passed the Pacific Railroad Act, authorizing construction of a transcontinental rail line on a northern route along the 42nd parallel

Below: An illustration from Frank Leslie's Magazine *of December 1869 portrays the crowd at a Union Pacific depot in San Francisco after the opening of the New York–San Francisco transcontinental line. The last spike, joining Union Pacific tracks with the Central Pacific Railroad, was hammered on May 10 of that year in Promontory, Utah.*

Below: Now in ruins, the silver-lead furnace at Owens Lake, California, was used in the nineteenth century for smelting, as part of the process of mining the valuable ore. Owens Lake is now dry, its water diverted by aqueduct to serve the city of Los Angeles.

instead. On May 10, 1869, the Union Pacific and Central Pacific Railroads met at Promontory Point, Utah. Other transcontinental routes quickly followed. The Southern Pacific entered Arizona in 1877. Then the Atlantic and Pacific—a subsidiary of the Atchison, Topeka & Santa Fe—met the Southern Pacific at Deming, New Mexico, in 1881. The Santa Fe, initially planned to run between Santa Fe, New Mexico, and Kansas City, Missouri, stretched all the way to San Francisco in the Northwest and eastward to Chicago.

Arrival of the Atchison, Topeka & Santa Fe line in Los Angeles in 1887 touched off a rates war with the Southern Pacific Railroad. The price-cutting that resulted helped fuel an influx of migration to California. In Los Angeles, railroads not only boosted population but provided the impetus to construction of a harbor for

the city at San Pedro. The new railroad lines built in the Southwest during the 1880s stemmed the great cattle drives by bringing rail depots closer to the cattle ranches, although cramped cattle cars and bad rail beds often injured the livestock. The Consolidated Land, Cattle Raising and Wool Growing Company of New Mexico and Colorado was incorporated in 1872 at $10 million. In Nevada, cattle ranching increased as the Comstock Lode diminished, although the cost of shipping by rail and the severe winters provided a built-in curb to the industry's growth.

As the nineteenth century came to a close, the Southwestern landscape featured railroads, oil fields, telephone lines, mining machinery, and other technological developments, but the inhabitants remained secure in their distinctive heritage and culture.

THE
TWENTIETH
CENTURY

Below: Hoover Dam, which spans the Colorado River in Black Canyon between Nevada and Arizona, is one of the great water diversion projects undertaken by the National Reclamation Bureau to create arable farmland in the Southwest and adjacent regions. Begun in 1931, it was named after the nation's 31st president, Herbert Hoover.

When the Southwest entered the twentieth century, three of the region's states—Oklahoma, Arizona, and New Mexico—were still territories. Oklahoma won statehood in 1907, while Arizona and New Mexico both joined the Union in 1912. Farming, mining, and cattle herding continued to dominate the region's economy, while oil and tourism would soon begin to gain in importance.

Although the nation's war with Mexico was a distant memory, one border clash with Mexico did occur early in the new century. In 1916 revolutionary Pancho Villa went on a killing and looting spree in Columbus, New Mexico, after the United States officially recognized his nation's new president. General John "Blackjack" Pershing led the American sortie into Mexico to punish Villa: he eluded capture, but most of his men were killed in the military venture.

The movement to transform the Southwest's deserts into agricultural oases had begun in the nineteenth century, but passage of the Newlands National Reclamation Act in 1902 sped up the process through formation of the National Reclamation Service, later renamed the National Reclamation Bureau. Southwestern land reclamation for agricultural use by irrigation also

provided electricity, flood control, recreation, and conservation. Farmers banded together in both national and regional organizations to support irrigation. The first projects were on the Salt River in Arizona, where in 1911 Theodore Roosevelt Dam rose 284 feet—the highest masonry dam of the time. Similar construction took place on the Truckee and Carson Rivers in Nevada.

Large parts of southern California, Nevada, and Arizona have average annual precipitation of less than 12 inches, while about half of the states of New Mexico, Oklahoma, and Texas get only up to 36 inches. Water rights— over who would gain access to the Colorado River—generated friction between California and Arizona in the twentieth century. The Colorado River Compact of 1922 resolved their conflict by apportioning water among these two states and five others. New fields of alfalfa, barley, cotton, sugar beets, wheat, beans, and sorghum appeared once water became available through diversion of the Colorado River. However, when William Mulholland—for whom Mulholland Drive in Los Angeles is named—built a 500-mile aqueduct to bring water from the Sierra Nevada Mountains to Los Angeles, Owens River Valley farmers tried to stop the diversion by dynamiting the aqueduct.

Built in 1916, Elephant Butte Dam on the Rio Grande in New Mexico created a lake forty miles long and three miles wide and supplied water for nearly 160,000 acres of farmland in New Mexico, Texas, and Mexico. Elwood Mead, who headed the National Reclamation Bureau from 1924 to 1936, was instrumental in building Hoover Dam on the Colorado River in Black Canyon,

between Nevada and Arizona. Construction of Hoover Dam started in 1931 and was completed in 1936. It was soon followed by the Imperial and Parker Dams. Imperial Dam, finished in 1938, directed water into the Imperial Valley for crops. Parker Dam, farther south on the Colorado River, provided water for Los Angeles, San Diego, and other parts of southern California.

When it came to reclamation and irrigation in the Southwest, progress was not always positive. The California Development Company opened a new intake for its canal feeding southern California's Imperial Valley just in time, unfortunately, for a series of winter floods in 1906. Floodwaters swamped the Southern Pacific's tracks and a nearby salt company. The railroad had to step in and dump thousands of carloads of fill to contain the damage. By 1907 the resulting lake had become so salty that the state stocked it with ocean fish. Dams succeeded at diverting water to arid land so that it could be farmed, but some were prone to silting up. The

Left: Canals such as the one pictured under construction here at Bosque Farms in New Mexico provided an alternative to the damming of rivers in the Southwest. This method of irrigation dates back to early Native American farming practices.

Page 113: A sun-bleached longhorn skull decorates a hand-hewn wagon wheel in the adobe courtyard at Fort Leaton State Historic Site in Texas. The trading post there was built in 1848 by Ben Leaton, who traded with Apache and Comanche Indians.

Overleaf: "The Temple" is one of the scenic rock formations at Lake Mead between Arizona and Nevada. The lake, created in 1935 by construction of Hoover Dam, was named after Elwood Mead, head of the National Reclamation Bureau from 1924 to 1936. It is one of the largest artificial lakes in the world.

Previous page:
Cactus and other vegetation typical of the Southwest's arid sections rise out of the Sonoran Desert at Organ Pipe Cactus National Monument in Arizona. Pictured are the Saguaro and the Organ Pipe Cacti, two of the largest of the species. On the horizon lie the Ajo Mountains.

Below: *Beef cattle look up from a feeding trough at Casa Grande Farms in Coolidge, Arizona. The year was 1942, and the Pinal County enterprise was a Farm Security Administration project.*

reservoirs behind them grew salty through concentration and evaporation. Water tables dropped when surface water ran out and ground water was pumped for irrigation. Pollution occurred from fertilizer and pesticide leaching.

Nor were the problems confined to the American stretch of the Colorado River. When ground water pumped to crops along the Colorado River was returned to the river, Mexican crops in the Mexicali Valley withered because of increased salinity. The year of the stock market crash, 1929, also marked the beginning of a ten-year drought cycle in the Great Plains states of the Southwest, Texas, and New Mexico. Many farmers moved to northern California, Oregon, or Washington, where rainfall reaches 40 inches yearly. There are no easy answers to the problems caused by water scarcity in the Southwest.

Water was less of an issue for Oklahoma farmers than was land acquisition. When it acquired territorial status in 1890, what was then Oklahoma contained seven counties. In addition, there were the Chickasaw Nation, Cherokee Outlet, and other Native American reservations. The latter were considered ripe for settlement at the time of the

last Oklahoma land lottery, which took place in 1905. What is now Oklahoma was still divided then into two territories, Oklahoma and Indian Territory. Each wanted separate statehood, and the two did not agree to combine until 1906, when enabling legislation was finally passed. The constitution drawn up for the new state was largely the work of populist reformer Kate Barnard, who went on to become the Commissioner of Charities and Corrections, the first woman elected to public office in Oklahoma. The capital was moved from Guthrie to Oklahoma City in 1910, and construction on a new capitol building was begun in 1914.

During the twentieth century, American subsistence farming, whereby each family produced enough for itself, went out with the horse and buggy. Agriculture became big business in the Southwest, thanks to irrigation, and in considerable part, to federal subsidy. Not only did the amount of acreage given to homesteaders quadruple by 1916, but the government levied tariffs like the one on sugar imports that supported the Southwest's sugar beet farmers. By mid-century, California was producing more than a third of the nation's vegetables excluding potatoes; more than a quarter of its berries and small fruit; and more than 42 percent of orchard fruit and nuts. The economics of twentieth-century, big-business agriculture in the Southwest dictated a need for better financing for farmers. Other problems faced by farmers included overproduction, soil erosion, soil exhaustion, the poverty created by tenant farming, and, finally, the advent of corporate agriculture that threatened to put the individual farmer out of business.

Mining continued to play an important part in development of the region. Copper and potash were two valuable Southwestern natural resources. The Arizona copper deposits mentioned earlier, at Bisbee, Globe, Jerome, and Clifton-Morenci were discovered in limestone deposits. Later, disseminated-ore deposits in low-grade porphyries were mined at Ely, Nevada; Santa Rita, New Mexico; and Ray, Arizona. Arizona has dominated the latter form of copper mining since 1907. Large deposits of potassium carbonate or potash, which is an important ingredient in fertilizers, were developed outside of Carlsbad, New Mexico, in the 1920s.

New mining towns like Searchlight, Nevada; Shakespeare, New Mexico; and Contention City, Texas, sprang up across the Southwest early in the century, their growth seeded by the great mining companies that controlled the ore, the housing, the businesses, even, in some cases, the libraries. Phelps Dodge built one

such town, Tyrone, Arizona, with its own railroad depot and company-owned housing. Unlike the mining towns of the nineteenth century, these were carefully planned and laid out by the companies who controlled the ore.

Open-pit techniques made mining of the Southwest's coal, iron, boron, gypsum, perlite, and sand far more efficient, if less environmentally friendly, in the new century. In Oklahoma, coal mining went hand in hand with the coming of the railroads. By 1906, after coal was discovered on Creek and Cherokee land, Oklahoma was producing 2.5 million tons of coal—nearly 1 percent of the nation's total. Carlsbad, Texas, still produces 85 percent of U.S. potash, while Boron, California, dominates in borax. The Southwest is rich in other minerals for which twentieth-century technology provided the extraction techniques, including salt, lead, and zinc. Uranium discoveries in the Colorado Plateau, which includes northern New Mexico

Above: *Residents of San Ildefonso Pueblo in New Mexico hang up chili ristras for drying in 1935. Ristra means "string" in Spanish, and chili ristras symbolize a plentiful harvest. San Ildefonso was the home of Maria Martinez, who developed black-on-black pottery. Her work is on view at the Pueblo's museum.*

Above: A display of early equipment used at Harmony Borax Works overlooks Death Valley, California. The mining company operated in the 1880s and was the first successful operation of its sort in Death Valley. Teams of twenty mules pulled up to 46,000-pound loads of borax to the railroad depot in Mojave.

and Arizona, led to mining of the ore in that section of the Southwest. Grants, New Mexico, became the uranium capital of the world after World War II. The number of uranium mines in the Southwest and parts of Colorado and Utah grew to 800 by 1955. During the first half of the twentieth century, uranium-rich New Mexico earned a dubious claim to fame by providing a venue for development of the first nuclear bomb, which was detonated on July 16, 1945, in Los Alamos.

If railroads opened up the Southwest to settlement and industry in the nineteenth century, they brought an influx of tourists in the twentieth. The Santa Fe Railroad, for instance, built a spur line in 1901 to the southern rim of the Grand Canyon. Las Vegas, Nevada, started out as a work camp for the Los Angeles–Salt Lake Railroad in 1903. The Harvey Girls, introduced by restaurateur Frederick H. Harvey, provided table service at Santa Fe Railroad hotels like the El Navajo in Gallup, New Mexico, and the Casa del

Desierto in Barstow, California. Rail travel was increasingly augmented by automobiles, particularly along the southern route known as the Ocean-to-Ocean Highway. Tourism led the Arizona economy by the 1930s, and topped New Mexico's economy as well after World War II, when money became available to build interstate highways. After gambling was legalized in Nevada in 1931, tourists flocked there, too, while Hollywood, with its movie studios and film palaces like Grauman's Chinese Theatre, attracted visitors to California.

In addition to tourism, the advent of the automobile in 1915 spurred development of the region's great cities, including Albuquerque, Phoenix, Las Vegas, and Dallas.

The mild climate drew still another group to the Southwest—retirees looking for permanent sunshine. El Paso, Texas, offers a prototype of the typical Southwestern city in the first half of the twentieth century. Its population had a large proportion of Mexicans, and it featured a frontier-vintage army post, Fort Bliss. El Paso sent workers into New Mexico and welcomed laborers from across the border with Mexico. Like so many American cities, it quickly spread out from its center to form that peculiarly twentieth-century phenomenon, the suburb.

Transportation advances lent new appeal to Southwestern deserts in particular. In addition to the wonders of Arizona's Grand Canyon, tourists could

Below: This mission-style railroad depot in Caliente, Nevada, opened in 1923. It served as Union Pacific's maintenance center until 1948. The restored building now houses Caliente's city hall, as well as the library, an art gallery and community college classrooms.

Above: *El Navajo Hotel in Gallup, New Mexico, was built to serve the Santa Fe Railroad and still operates. It was designed by architect Mary E. J. Colter, who worked for the Fred Harvey Company, which built and staffed many similar railroad accommodations.*

now visit New Mexico's gypsum dunes of White Sands and the Carlsbad Caverns; Arizona's Chiricahua Mountains, with their Casas Grandes ruins; and California's Death Valley. Artifacts of the Southwest's rich Native-American cultural heritage attracted many visitors to the region's states. The matte-black pottery made by Maria Gonzales and her family at San Ildefonso, New Mexico, offers only one example. Anglo artists who flocked to Taos, New Mexico, and to Georgia O'Keeffe's home nearby, turned that pueblo-based community into a mecca for art lovers. Frank Lloyd Wright's architectural school, started in 1938 as Taliesin West, in Scottsdale, Arizona, attracted eager students and architects alike.

After the advent of barbed wire in the last decades of the nineteenth century and the fence wars that ensued, cattle ranching in Texas and Arizona found itself increasingly regulated by the federal government and subject to greater controls over grazing on public lands. The early boom years were over. Beef

prices dropped 50 percent over a five-year period, starting in 1918. By 1931 prices had dropped by 66 percent. Moreover, drought plagued ranchers so severely in the early 1920s that by 1934 President Roosevelt's New Dealers had established the Drought Relief Service to buy up cattle and reduce herds. The Taylor Grazing Act of 1934 put almost all public lands under federal control. The Bureau of Land Management took control of public grazing land in 1946 and began restricting use of environmentally sensitive areas. It also encouraged herd reduction. In the years after World War II, the cattle industry saw another boom period, and larger cattle ranches bought out their smaller neighbors. Between 1940 and 1950, medium-sized ranches increased by 20 percent.

Like cattle ranching, the Texas and Oklahoma oil industry became big business in the twentieth century. By 1920 Oklahoma was producing over 106 million barrels of crude oil, more than California or Texas. As oil production decreased along the Gulf Coast in the first part of the new century, the companies that preceded Texaco and Gulf built pipelines to both Oklahoma and Texas's mid-continent oil fields. Sinclair, Phillips, Cities Service, and Skelly joined the competition with Standard, which dominated in California but had been hit with an anti-trust suit in 1911, along with its California competitors, Union and Associated. Royal Dutch Shell moved into the California oil business in 1913. Before the turn of the century, the oil industry's primary product had been kerosene. By 1910 the automobile had changed that equation. Crude oil and, eventually, gasoline became the industry's primary products.

Cheap oil fueled industrialization of the Southwest's new cities from Los Angeles to Houston. These new urban areas had a different character than older cities in the East. Growing up at the same time as the automobile, they spilled out into rambling suburbs. The best-known Southwestern suburb is probably Scottsdale, Arizona, outside of Phoenix. So abundant became the supplies of oil that in 1928 the Oklahoma Corporation Commission capped production at 700,000 barrels per diem, although many oil companies simply ignored the Commission. By 1931 overproduction at the nation's largest oil field, East Texas, pushed prices below 10 cents a barrel.

In 1933 the New Deal's National Recovery Administration started to curb the flood of oil generated by unregulated production, but it was declared unconstitutional in 1935. The Interstate Oil Compact that replaced it put production quotas into effect. As the oil industry developed an ever-new range of petroleum products, the demand for oil grew. In California, the coast north of Los Angeles, the Los Angeles Basin area, and the San Joaquin Valley have been prime targets in the hunt for new oil. The search for oil also went on in all of Texas, New Mexico— where oil wasn't discovered until the 1920s—and Oklahoma. Although offshore drilling in California dates back to 1894 in the Santa Barbara Channel, and at Black Duck Bay in Texas (1917), it wasn't until the 1930s that technological development permitted sustained offshore drilling. Air travel further fueled the demand for oil.

With the advent of both the automobile and the airplane, twentieth-century transportation changed the face of the Southwest. At the end of the nineteenth century, railroads had dominated national and regional life, but not always in positive ways. Gouging farmers for shipping charges and lobbying for special favors from legislators, the railroad industry incurred the public's wrath, and Congress considered regulation. The Interstate Commerce and Sherman Anti-trust Acts put the fear of God into the industry. In the first

Below: The metal riggings of oil derricks, dating from 1943, create the appearance of an urban landscape in Kilgore, Texas. The East Texas Oil Museum is located in Kilgore, which once was an oil boom town.

Right: Downtown Reno, Nevada, with its famous arch that heralds "The Biggest Little City in the World." The original iron arch spanning Virginia Street was built in 1928, and was replaced by the one pictured.

Opposite: Snow festoons the peaceful shoreline of Lake Tahoe at Sand Harbor State Park in Nevada, now the home of the Shakespeare at Sand Harbor festival. Lake Tahoe straddles both Nevada and California.

decade of the new century, most railroads were rebuilt. Edward Ripley and Victor Morawetz turned the Santa Fe from a pieced-together, ramshackle enterprise into a first-class operation.

Long before the automobile was introduced, the federal government had begun considering a national highway—and canal—system. Starting in the 1830s, military roads provided the earliest "modern" routes through the Southwest. One went from Fort Smith, Arkansas, to Albuquerque, New Mexico; another, from San Antonio, Texas, to San Diego,

California, with several interruptions. The great distances involved in crossing the Southwest made construction of a highway system with limited access, no traffic lights, and no cross streets a high priority. Although paving was accomplished, a national highway system did not crisscross the region until the 1960s, primarily using old pioneer traces like the Santa Fe and Chihuahua Trails. But beginning in the late 1930s, California led efforts to build major highway systems for its cities, and many state roads had been converted to freeways and express-

Above: Vintage gas stations such as this one dating from 1939 at Edcouch, Texas, lacked the amenities modern drivers have become accustomed to. The town was named after local landowner Edward Couch.

ways by the late 1950s. San Francisco's Embarcadero Freeway (I-480)—since torn down—was built in 1959.

The airplane age arrived in the Southwest in 1911, when Calbraith P. Rodgers completed the first transcontinental flight from New York to Pasadena, California. (It took him forty-nine days, but only some eighty-two hours were spent in the air!) By 1921 the nation's first transcontinental airmail service made stops in Reno, Nevada, and San Francisco, California. Trans-World Airline's first route included Albuquerque, New Mexico, and continued across Arizona to Los Angeles. United Airlines took a more northerly route into San Francisco, and American Airlines' earliest trips went from Cleveland to Fort Worth, Texas. Los Angeles International Airport began as Mines Field in 1928 and has gone on to become the world's fourth-busiest airport. In Texas, Dallas first proposed joining forces with Fort Worth to build a major airport in 1927, but Fort Worth wasn't interested. The Civil Aeronautics Administration got involved in the rivalry in 1940, but the Dallas/Fort Worth International Airport didn't take shape until 1974.

The mobility that automobile and air travel gave Americans, as well as twentieth-century conservation concerns, encouraged development of the National Park and Monument system in the Southwest. Arizona designated the Indian cliff dwellings in the Salt River Valley as the Tonto National Monument in 1907. Canyon de Chelly National Monument was established in northeast Arizona in 1911 to preserve Indian ruins dating from c. AD 350 to 1300. Casas Grande National Monument in south-central Arizona offers examples of early native buildings and canals. Chiricahua National Monument in the southeastern section of the state, named for an Apache tribe, came into existence in 1924. Sunset Crater Volcano National Monument near Flagstaff was established in 1930; Grand Canyon, declared a national monument in 1908, first became a national park in 1932. Coronado National Memorial near Nogales was built in 1952 to celebrate the 400th anniversary of the Spanish explorer's travels through the state.

Southern California has Cabrillo National Monument, named for the sixteenth-century Spanish explorer, which now features a historic lighthouse. Joshua Tree National Monument, with its unique desert vegetation, was established in 1936 near Indio. Other California national monuments and parks include the volcanic spires of Pinnacles National Monument near Hollister; Channel Islands National Park, first established in 1938 as a national monument; and Death Valley National Park, which began in 1933 as a national monument. Yosemite National Park, the nation's oldest, was established by Congress in 1890, as mentioned earlier.

Nevada had only one such reserve during the first half of the twentieth century in Lehman Caves, which was a national monument until it was incorporated into Great Basin National Park, established in 1986. The northeast corner of Death Valley National Monument is also in Nevada. Nevada's oldest state park, Valley of Fire, was dedicated in 1935. Located outside of Las Vegas, it was named for its red sandstone formations, including one named Elephant Rock. It also contains native petroglyphs.

In New Mexico, the writings on Inscription Rock at El Morro National Monument, established in 1906, date back to Spanish colonizer Juan de Oñate. Chaco Culture National Historical Park, containing the ruins of thirteen ancient Native-American cities, became a New Mexico national monument in 1907, and Gila Cliff Dwellings National Monument was established the same year. Gran Quivira National Monument was named in 1909 because of its Spanish Franciscan missions and is now part of Salinas Pueblo Missions National Monument. Native American cave rooms have been preserved at Bandelier National Monument since 1916, and the volcanic cone of Capulin Mountain was made a national monument in 1916. One of the largest prehistoric pueblos became Aztec Ruins National Monument in 1923. Filled with stalagmites and stalactites, Carlsbad Caverns National Park (established in 1923) contains one of the largest caves in the world.

Oklahoma is home to only one national historic site, the Washita Battlefield, where General George Armstrong Custer massacred an encampment of Cheyenne in 1868. West Texas's Big Bend National Park began

as a state park in 1933; the enlarged national park was authorized in 1935. Alibates Flint Quarries National Monument in Texas marks the site of the agatized dolomite deposits used by prehistoric Native Americans to make knives and other stone implements.

The twentieth century also witnessed the development of the Southwest's great institutions of higher education, as well as its renowned scientific and cultural centers. Among the most prominent are, in California, the University of Southern California at Los Angeles, the Henry Huntington Library at Pasadena, Mount Wilson Observatory, and the Hollywood Bowl; the University of Oklahoma at Norman and Oklahoma State University at Stillwater; the University of Nevada at Reno; in Arizona, the University of Arizona and Kitt Peak National Observatory; and the University of Texas at the state capital in Austin.

By the mid-twentieth century, the Southwest could no longer be stereotyped as cowboy and cactus country. Both these icons remained symbols of the region, but they had been joined by massive agricultural enterprises, the mining, oil, and tourist industries that fueled a thriving economy, and a richly diverse culture that maintained pride in its own character while contributing mightily to the United States of America.

Overleaf: A dramatic sunset in Saguaro National Monument, in southern Arizona, silhouettes two saguaro cacti against the skyline. The giant cactus has been protected within Saguaro National Park since the 1930s.

Below: Workers' automobiles are lined up in a parking lot for a San Diego, California, airplane factory in 1940. Many of the vehicles date from much earlier because of wartime restrictions on producing private vehicles.

SOUTHERN CALIFORNIA

LOS ANGELES AND THE SOUTH

Los Angeles

El Pueblo de Los Angeles Historic Monument: preserved center of the old Spanish Settlement; includes the ***Avila Adobe***, a reconstructed 1818 adobe replicating a Mexican cattleman's home of the 1840s; and the ***Plaza Substation***, a 1904 power station for the streetcar system

Southwest Museum: The oldest museum in Los Angeles, formed in 1907, with displays of Native American artifacts, including basketry; also maintains the ***Casa de Adobe***, a re-created pre-1850s Spanish Colonial hacienda

City Hall: offers spectacular city views

Wells Fargo History Museum: replica gold-rush-era Wells Fargo office; collection of stagecoaches; Dorsey gold collection

Coca-Cola Building: architectural landmark

California State Museum of Science and Industry: exhibits include satellites, rockets, the human body, and the history of the state's industry

Natural History Museum of Los Angeles County: renowned displays on pre-Columbian Meso-American culture, and the history of the state and area

George C. Page Museum of La Brea Discoveries: huge paleontological collection dug from tar pits, including about 100,000 fossils; also displays preserved remains of over 200 different species, many extinct; includes sloths, mammoths, camels, birds, even a 9,000-year-old female body recovered from the tar pits

Museum of Contemporary Arts: paintings and sculptures by the rising stars of American art

Hollywood

Studio Museum: housed in the first movie studio in Hollywood, exhibits on the history of motion pictures

Hollywood Sign: famous landmark, erected 1923

Mann's Chinese Theater: contains the famous forecourt of signatures, handprints, and footprints of many Hollywood stars since its opening in the 1920s as Grauman's Chinese Theater

Egyptian Theater: opened in 1922 as a re-creation of the Temple of Thebes

Hollywood Memorial Park Cemetery: final resting place of many early stars, including Rudolph Valentino

Coastside

Malibu: beach resort and Malibu Creek State Park, previously owned and used by Twentieth Century Fox for scenery

Santa Monica: beach resort with a 1920s pier; also contains the California Heritage Museum, in an 1890s house

Venice: historic beach site, founded 1904; thriving arts scene

Will Rogers State Historic Park: preserved ranch house and park of the Rogers family; walking trails and scenic views

J. Paul Getty Museum: huge museum complex in 110-acre area of gardens, fountains, and pools; includes a permanent collection of international fine and decorative art

Wayfarers Chapel: designed by Frank Lloyd Wright and completed in 1951; made almost entirely of glass, it offers commanding ocean views; contains exhibits on Swedenborgianism

San Pedro
Cabrillo Marine Aquarium: southern Californian marine life
Los Angeles Maritime Museum: walk-in naval exhibits

Long Beach
Queen Mary: huge, retired British ocean liner, completely refurbished in Art Deco style; now a hotel and museum
El Dorado Nature Center: wildlife sanctuary and museum
Long Beach Museum of Art: excellent modern art collection
Rancho Los Cerritos Historic Site: preserved mid-nineteenth-century adobe and ranch gardens, with tours, lectures, and interactive historical programs

Santa Catalina Island
Catalina Island Museum: housed in the Wrigley's 1929 Casino Building; exhibits the island's history, photographs, and artifacts
Santa Monica Mountains National Recreation Area: has a full range of outdoor activities
Channel Islands National Park: plants, animals, and marine life abound as a setting for many outdoor activities and watersports

SAN GABRIEL VALLEY

Pasadena
Gamble House: definitive example of the Arts and Crafts movement; remarkable interior and exterior design; open for visitors
Pasadena Historical Society: house museum, cultural museum, and Finnish folk-arts museum
Norton Simon Museum of Art: European paintings, sculpture, and tapestries; also Asian sculpture collection spanning 2,000 years

San Gabriel
Mission San Gabriel Archangel: founded 1771 with interesting Spanish Colonial church; historical reconstructions

San Marino
The Huntingdon Library, Art Collections and Botanical Gardens: World-famous collection of eighteenth- and nineteenth-century British and French painting and decorative arts; the library also contains many valuable rare manuscripts and books

Arcadia
Los Angeles State and County Arboretum: 127-acre garden of exotic flora and fauna; children's cultural workshops

Industry
Workman and Temple Homestead Museum: commemorates the first overland settlement expedition pioneers; includes restored homes with original furnishings; offers interpretive tours

SAN FERNANDO VALLEY

Glendale
Forest Lawn Memorial Park: famous cemetery with full-scale reproductions of public buildings and paintings

Burbank
Gordon R. Howard Museum: antique automobiles; life-size vignettes of local history

Mission Hills
Mission San Fernando Rey de España: founded in 1797; includes collection of artifacts from the high point of the mission era

NORTHERN LOS ANGELES COUNTY

Newhall
Vásquez Rocks County Park: preserves huge sandstone rock formations and incised petroglyphs
William S. Hart County Park and Museum: estate of Hollywood's first cowboy movie star; preserved as he left it

Paicines
Pinnacles National Monument: remains of an ancient volcano; plants and animals of a typical chaparral community

EASTERN LOS ANGELES COUNTY

San Bernardino
The Arrowhead: a legendary prehistoric landmark—a huge, arrow-shaped design incised on the side of a mountain

Riverside
Riverside Municipal Museum: exhibits and artifacts on local history from the pre-Columbian period to Spanish exploration
Jensen-Alvarado Ranch: restored as a living-history farm
March Field Museum: vintage aircraft, memorabilia, photographs, and uniforms

Redlands
Historical Glass Museum: history of American glassware
Lincoln Memorial Shrine: important collection of Lincoln memorabilia—books, pamphlets, portraits, and busts

Hemet
Maze Stone Park: Indian Petroglyph site

Three Rivers
Sequoia and King's Canyon National Parks: giant trees, high peaks, and deep canyons; has camping facilities, 700 miles of hiking trails, fishing, skiing, horseback riding, exhibits

ORANGE COUNTY

Yorba Linda
Richard Nixon Presidential Library and Birthplace: complex commemorating the 37th president of the United States

San Diego
Old Point Loma Lighthouse: open for tours; excellent views
Maritime Museum: three vintage ships refitted and restored
Seeley Stables: museum of horse-drawn vehicles and equipment
William Heath Davis House and Museum: 140-year-old house and the oldest structure in "New Town"; offers tours of the area including gaslamp walking tours and the Wyatt Earp Tour
Balboa Park: center for the city's museums; contains twelve facilities including: the San Diego Zoo, Museum of Man, San Diego Museum of Art, Timken Art Gallery, San Diego Natural History Museum, a space theater and science center
Mission Basilica San Diego de Alcala: restored mission with a museum of Native American arts and relics
Cabrillo National Monument: marks site of the first landing of Juan Rodriguez Cabrillo's voyage; outdoor activities including nature and whale watching, tidepools, and guided walks

SAN DIEGO COUNTY

San Luis Rey
Mission San Luis Rey de Francia: the largest and most populous of the California missions; elaborate, with a restored church and the state's oldest pepper tree

San Pasqual Battlefield State Historic Park
Significant Mexican War battle site of 1846 with a visitor center

Julian
Julian Pioneer Museum: artifacts of mining era
Eagle Mining Company: tours of two old mines
San Diego Railroad Museum: reconstructed Victorian depot with 1920s rolling stock collection; train rides

THE SOUTHERN DESERT

Palm Springs
Village Green Heritage Center: historic artifacts
Agua Caliente Culture Museum: interprets the history of the local Native Americans
Desert Museum: Native American and Southwestern art and natural-science exhibition

Blythe
Indian Lore Monument: large intaglios of men and animals, more than 5,000 years old, carved into the rock

Anza-Borrego Desert States Park
A massive park of passes and canyons marking important routes into California; the Borrego Valley contains the *Vallecitos Stage Depot*, an authentic reconsruction of an 1852 stage stop

The Mojave Desert
Sparsely populated region; geologically interesting with dramatic landscapes; meets the Colorado Desert at the *Joshua Tree National Monument*; range of outdoor activities

Death Valley National Park
120-mile-long valley featuring the *Furnace Creek Visitor Center*, which contains historical and geological exhibits of the area; also contains *Badwater*, the lowest point in the United States, and *Scotty's Castle*, a Mediterranean-style complex built by the flamboyant "Death Valley Scotty" and open for tours

Death Valley National Monument
The hottest place in North America, but it has a varied plantlife; the monument comprises a wide area of snow-covered peaks, sand dunes, and abandoned mines, where tours are available

Calico
Calico Early Man Site: archaeological site of contested date; many thousands of finds; tours available
Calico Ghost Town: reconstructed mining town that was once well populated; mineshaft tours available

Mojave
Red Rock Canyon: classic movie location of richly colored cliffs

White Mountains
Home to the bristlecone pines, the oldest living things on earth, some more than 4, 000 years old

Victorville
Roy Rogers and Dale Evans Museum: unusual family collections of guns, dolls, transport models, and movie memorabilia, including Rogers' mounted dog and horse

Randsburg
Randsburg Historical Museum: photographs and mining artifacts, set in a tiny rustic mining town

Ridgecrest
Maturango Museum: offers tours of the naval weapons center and Petroglyph Canyon where some of the many petroglyphs are more than 10,000 years old; a museum of cultural and natural history and geology of the north Mojave Desert area

ARIZONA

SOUTHERN ARIZONA

Tucson

Tucson Museum of Art: features pre-Columbian and Western works; gives access to El Presidio and its historic adobe homes

Sosa-Carrillo-Frémont House: 1860s adobe house with period features and Victorian furnishings

University Museum of Art: features an excellent collection of sculpture; Renaissance and seventeenth-century European masterpieces; and some valuable American pieces

Arizona State Museum: early Native American artifacts

Arizona Historical Society Museum: thousands of artifacts and photographs; many re-created scenes, predominantly from the mining era, and period rooms

Saguaro National Park: preserves the ancient and enormous Saguaro cacti

Pima Air and Space Museum: the largest private air museum, containing a huge collection of historic aircraft

Fort Lowell Museum: displays artifacts from this important army post, established in 1866

Mission San Xavier del Bac: eighteenth-century church and mission of elaborate interior decoration; the best-preserved mission church in the United States

Amerind Foundation

An archaeological research facility and museum of excavated artifacts, mainly native craftwork

Fort Bowie National Historical Site

Commemorates the scene of Chiricahua Apache and U.S. military conflict and the site of Geronimo's surrender; visitors find the stabilized ruins of the former army stronghold guarding Apache Pass

Chiricahua National Monument

Contains huge and extraordinary rock formations with a visitor center on the area's geology and history; also offers range of outdoor activities

Bisbee

Queen Mine: offers tours of a large open-pit copper mine

Bisbee Mining and Historical Museum: preserved headquarters of the late-nineteenth-century Copper Queen Consolidated Mining Company; exhibits photographs and equipment

Tombstone

Crystal Palace Saloon: restored to its original appearance of 1879

Bird Cage Theater: notorious theater, saloon, and brothel, preserved with original fixtures from 1881, including 140 bullet holes

Tombstone Courthouse State Historic Park: scene of legendary local trials and hangings; the 1882 courthouse is now a museum

O.K. Corral: scene of legendary gunfight involving the Earp brothers and "Doc" Holliday

Coronado National Memorial

Commemorates the historic trek of Coronado in 1540 to find the fabled Seven Cities of Cibola; contains museum and visitor center with exhibits relating to the trek; also offers spectacular and unspoilt views of the river valley and hiking up to the Coronado Peak

Tubac

Tubac Presidio State Historic Park: Archaeological excavation site of a 1750s commandant's house with an interpretive visitor center and viewing gallery

Colonial Tubac Archaeological Park: large number of colonial ruins and still-active excavations

Tumacacori National Historical Park

Eighteenth-century mission outpost with Spanish Colonial Baroque church, museum, and gardens

Oracle

Biosphere 2: the giant plexiglass bubble is a working model of Earth; site of the 1991 experiment in which eight people were to be locked inside for two years; guided tours available

SOUTH-CENTRAL ARIZONA

Casa Grande Ruins National Monument

The largest Hohokam Indian building, dated c.1320, perhaps used for astronomical observation; contains an interpretive visitor center and guided trails

Florence

Pinal County Historical Museum: exhibits relating to the local prison, including implements of execution

Globe

Gila County Historical Museum: reproduces a section of an early underground mine; displays period rooms and artifacts from the *Besh-Ba-Gowah Ruins*, the home of the Salado Indians from 1225 to 1400

Tonto National Monument

Cliff dwellings of the Salado Indians in the mid-fourteenth century; visitor center offers a trail tour to the Lower Ruin

Apache Trail

Previously an Apache warpath, now a scenic road through the Superstition Wilderness, it passes *Weaver's Needle*, a 4,553-foot pinnacle and prospectors' landmark, and the *Roosevelt Dam*, the highest masonry dam in the world, completed in 1911

Phoenix

Arizona State Capitol Museum: 1899 building of the territorial capitol, restored to its appearance in 1912

Heard Museum: thousands of objects displayed to represent Southwestern culture from prehistoric times to the present

Pueblo Grande Museum: features the excavation of the Hohokam civilization of desert farmers of the eighth to the fourteenth centuries

Tempe

Tempe Historical Museum: follows the story of water development in the desert, and the local history of Hohokam Indians, farming, commerce, and industry

Scottsdale

Taliesen West: winter headquarters for the architect Frank Lloyd Wright's home and studio—completed 1938; now serves as an architectural archive for the Frank Lloyd Wright Foundation

Rawhide: a re-creation of a Western town with some twenty-five replica buildings from the 1880s; also contains a historical museum, cowboy shootouts, train rides, and stunt shows

Wickenburg

Desert Caballeros Western Museum: period rooms; an early street scene; Native American exhibits; mining dioramas; and Western art

Yuma

Arizona Historical Society/Century House Museum and Gardens: photographs and artifacts; aviary; and extensive gardens

Yuma Territorial Prison State Historic Park: 1876 prison built on the banks of the Colorado River with dungeons carved from solid rock; open for visitors with a museum of photographs and stories of various prisoners

ARIZONA STRIP

Page

John Wesley Powell Memorial Museum: commemorates the Civil War major who led the first expedition down the Colorado River and through the Grand Canyon; includes photographs, artifacts, arts, and crafts; offers river and lake trips, scenic flights, and local tours

Pipe Springs National Monument

Restored 1871 ranch house called Winsor Castle; demonstrations of pioneer crafts; and visitor center

Grand Canyon National Park

Tours, hiking, horseback riding, and water activities are offered in this famous landscape. Apart from merely viewing the spectacle, visitors may also see the *Grand Canyon Village*, an official historic district with buildings of interest; *Buckley O'Neill Cabin*, the oldest surviving structure on the canyon rim, built 1890s; *Desert View Watchtower*, the highest point on the South Rim with spectacular views; and *Tusayan Ruin*, an Anasazi site from the late twelfth century

THE NAVAJO RESERVATION

Ganado

Hubbell Trading Post National Historic Site: situated on the Navajo Reservation, this nineteenth-century trading post is the oldest that was operated continuously, and is preserved with original Navajo wares

Canyon De Chelly National Monument
Cliffs 1,000 feet high, with Anasazi adobe dwellings; an official Navajo guide is required

Navajo National Monument
Over 700 prehistoric sites; an Anasazi dwelling place of the thirteenth century; *Keet Seel*, a preserved cliff-palace of 155 rooms, with occupation dating from the tenth century; *White House Ruins*, a large dwelling; *Mummy Cave*, the largest ruin in the monument; and *Antelope House*, a village featuring cliff paintings, possibly dated 1830s

Window Rock
Navajo Tribal Museum: arts, crafts, and exhibits of Navajo history

The Hopi Reservation
Visits only with a Hopi guide and permission from the Cultural Preservation Office
First Mesa: contains the villages of Hano, Sichomovi, and Walpi, an ancient pueblo
Second Mesa: contains the village of Shongopovi and the Hopi Cultural Center, which exhibits silver, basketry, weaving, kachina dolls, pottery, and photographs
Third Mesa: contains the village of Old Oraibi, inhabited since 1150, Hotevilla, and Bacabi

CENTRAL ARIZONA

Petrified Forest National Park
Puerco Ruin: a seventy-five-room dwelling, occupied from 1100 to 1400; petroglyphs
Agate House: a seven-room pueblo built of petrified wood, with reconstructed rooms
Newspaper Rock: a viewpoint of the park with a good collection of petroglyphs

Prescott
Sharlot Hall Museum and Historical Society: collection of nine historic buildings and four gardens, including the Governor's Mansion, Fort Misery, the School House, and the Ranch House—all dating from the late-nineteenth and early-twentieth centuries

Jerome
Sliding Jail: famous for sliding 225 feet from its original building site
Jerome Historical Society Museum: photographs and mining memorabilia
Jerome State Historic Park: state museum in the 1916 Douglas Mansion; offers good views of the town and valley

Flagstaff
Riordan State Historic Park: a forty-room log mansion, built in 1904, with original furnishings
Pioneer Historical Museum: photographs, logging and pioneer tools and artifacts
Museum of Northern Arizona: archaeology, ethnology, geology, art, and crafts from the Colorado Plateau
Lowell Observatory: founded 1894; visitor center with exhibits
Sunset Crater Volcano National Monument: dormant volcano formed in 1064; visitor center, and Lava Flow Trail
Walnut Canyon National Monument: twenty-five prehistoric cliff-dwellings; visitor center with displays of pottery and artifacts
Wupatki National Monument: includes the *Wupatki Ruin*, a pueblo approximately dated 1120; *Wukoki*, a beautifully constructed three-story pueblo; *Citadel*, an imposing two-story pueblo; *Nalakihu Ruin*, a ten-room excavation; and *Lomaki Ruin*, a beautiful pueblo dated c.1192

Kingman
Mohave Museum of History and Arts: re-created Mohave and Hualapai dwellings

Tuzigoot National Monument
Three large pueblo ruins, partly reconstructed, inhabited from the twelfth century until c.1425; a trail leads through the ruins; the lookout tower offers views of the Verde Valley; visitor center with prehistoric collections

Montezuma Castle National Monument
Twelfth-century, five-story Sinagua cliff dwellings

Fort Verde State Historic Park
The primary base for General George Crook, this late-nineteenth-century military camp has original buildings, furnishings, parade ground, and a small museum

Whiteriver
Fort Apache Museum: photographs of the nearby military camp founded in 1870; walking tours
Kinishba Ruins: early pueblo, excavated in the 1930s, believed to have had a large population in the 1300s

NEW MEXICO

NORTHERN NEW MEXICO

Santa Fe

Museum of Fine Arts: predominantly local contemporary and historic work

Palace of the Governors: continuously used since 1610; now a historical museum of archaeology and re-created period rooms

Santuario de Guadalupe: restored mission church; museum, art gallery, and performing arts center

Camino Lejo Museum Complex: contains the Museum of International Folk Art, Museum of Indian Arts and Culture, and the Wheelright Museum of the American Indian

Pecos

Pecos National Historic Park: ruins of the fifteenth-century pueblo; two Spanish missions; many other archaeological sites, a visitor center, and trails through the ruins

Santa Clara Pueblo

Puye Cliff Dwellings: constructed between AD 600 and c.1580

El Rancho De Las Golondrinas

A living-history museum of original ranch buildings, re-creations of early New Mexican buildings, and relocated structures

Chimayo

Santuario de Chimayo: twin-towered adobe church

Los Alamos

Los Alamos County Historical Museum: exhibits on the Los Alamos Ranch School and the Manhattan Project

Fuller Lodge Art Center: exhibits work of New Mexico artists

Bradbury Science Museum: part of the Los Alamos National Laboratory, the nation's main center for nuclear research

Bandelier National Monument

Scenic area of volcanic rock formations, Anasazi ruins, and pre-historic dwellings; visitor center and hiking trails

San Juan Pueblo

Many buildings dated from the 1300s and restored; artwork, dances, and ceremonies open to the public

Jemez State Monument

Historical pueblo ruins of Guisewa and San José de los Jemez; visitor center and museum

Chaco Culture National Historical Park

Preserved complex of more than 2,000 Anasazi ruins, inhabited from the tenth century; visitor center with films and exhibits

Aztec

Aztec Museum: artifacts and town memorabilia

Aztec Ruins National Monument: Anasazi ruins of a 500-room pueblo, constructed around 1110; restored kiva

Bloomfield

Salmon Ruin: Anasazi site from the late eleventh century

Chama

Cumbres & Toltec Scenic Railroad: sixty-four-mile, narrow-gauge, steam-driven line to Antonio, Colorado, dating from the 1880s

Taos

Ernest L. Blumenschein Home: adobe home dating partly from the 1790s; original furnishings and artwork exhibitions

La Hacienda de Don Antonio Severino Martinez: adobe home with period furnishings and exhibitions

Mission San Francisco de Asis: Franciscan church built late 1700s

Taos Pueblo: multi-storied historic pueblo

Millicent Rogers Museum: superb local art and crafts

Cimarron

Old Mill Museum: extensive collection of local artifacts

Raton

Downtown Historical District: buildings dating from 1879

Fort Union National Monument
The largest fort in the Southwest; tours and a museum

Las Vegas
Old Town Plaza: historic district
Roughriders' Memorial and City Museum: Commemorates the Roughriders' New Mexican headquarters

Madrid
Old Coal Mine Museum: view down mine shaft; exhibits

SOUTHERN NEW MEXICO

Albuquerque
Church of San Felipe de Neri: built 1793
New Mexico Museum of Natural History: full-scale animated models, fossils, and other archaeological finds
Sandia Crest: 10,500-foot forested peaks; skiing, scenic drives, world's largest single-span tramway; aerial tram
Indian Pueblo Cultural Center: pueblo history museum and contemporary arts and crafts market
Rio Grande Botanic Garden: rare desert plants

Petroglyph National Monument
Large displays of Native American rock art in a volcanic landscape, with more than 15,000 petroglyphs

Coronado State Monument
Multistoried Rio Grande pueblo called Kuaua; trail and visitor center with original frescoes and prehistoric murals

Pueblo of Isleta
Established in first half of thirteenth century; encompasses the 1720 Mission of Saint Augustine; several dances are performed annually

Acoma Pueblo
Also called Sky City, a historic pueblo

El Morro National Monument
Remains of the 1275 Atsinna Pueblo; 200-foot *Inscription Rock,* where drawings and writings are left by passersby

Truth or Consequences
Geronimo Springs Museum: Mimbres pottery and local history of the hot, healing springs

Silver City
Silver City Museum: excellent collection of photographs, artifacts, antiques, and craftworks

Gila Cliff Dwellings National Monument
An ancient pueblo inhabited since about 1280; boyhood home of Geronimo (Goyathlay), Apache leader; self-guided trail

Columbus
Pancho Villa State Park: site of a historic 1915 attack by the Mexican revolutionary leader, with original camp buildings

Las Cruces
White Sands National Monument: undulating dunes of pure gypsum; 16-mile round-trip drive; visitor center with exhibits

Deming
Deming Luna Mimbres Museum: pottery, baskets, artifacts

Alamogordo
New Mexico Museum of Space History: museum includes the International Space Hall of Fame, with suits, vehicles, and craft

Three Rivers
Three Rivers Petroglyph Site: thousands of petroglyphs

Lincoln State Memorial
Commemorating the town's history from the time of Billy the Kid; preserved buildings; period reconstructions

Salinas Pueblo Missions National Monument
Quarai: 1628 mission, chapel and Native American pueblo
Abó: ruins of the beautiful Mission of San Gregorio de Abó
Gran Quivira: prehistoric pueblo and mission church

Fort Sumner State Monument
Stronghold of Kit Carson; *Billy the Kid's Grave*

Roswell
Historical Center for Southeast New Mexico: set in a 1910 stately home, an incredible array of antiques and artifacts
International UFO Museum and Research Center
Roswell Museum and Art Center

Carlsbad Caverns National Park
A gigantic complex of subterranean chambers

Hobbs
Confederate Air Force Museum: collection of World War II aircraft, land vehicles, engines, and artifacts, preserved in perfect working condition

TEXAS

NORTH AND EAST TEXAS

Dallas

Thanksgiving Square: meditation garden, descending walkways, fountains, and modern chapel.

Dallas Museum of Art: European Impressionist paintings, contemporary sculpture, and workshops

Morton H. Meyerson Symphony Center: designed by I. M. Pei

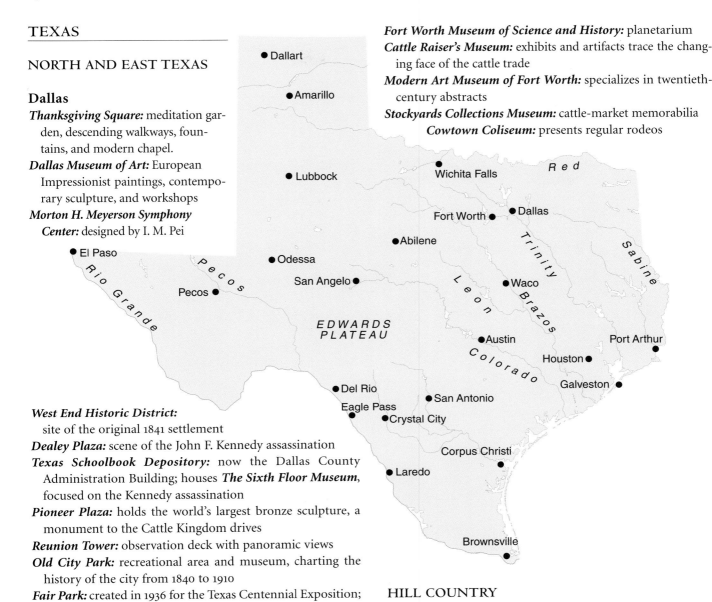

West End Historic District: site of the original 1841 settlement

Dealey Plaza: scene of the John F. Kennedy assassination

Texas Schoolbook Depository: now the Dallas County Administration Building; houses **The Sixth Floor Museum**, focused on the Kennedy assassination

Pioneer Plaza: holds the world's largest bronze sculpture, a monument to the Cattle Kingdom drives

Reunion Tower: observation deck with panoramic views

Old City Park: recreational area and museum, charting the history of the city from 1840 to 1910

Fair Park: created in 1936 for the Texas Centennial Exposition; annual Texas State Fair; museums; science center; planetarium; and an African-American Museum

Fort Worth

"Wall Street of the West": the Fort Worth Livestock Exchange; includes museum of photos and memorabilia

Sundance Square: notable for its public art, particularly the *trompe l'oeil* Chisholm Trail mural.

Sid Richardson Collection of Western Art: small collection of late works by Frederic Remington, including black-and-white illustrations, and early landscapes by Charles Russell

Kimbell Art Museum: displays of pre-Columbian and African pieces; European art; a seventh-century Khmer figure of a Hindu deity; and ancient Chinese bronzes, among other Asian pieces

Amon Carter Museum: includes photographs of Western landscapes and works by Georgia O'Keeffe

Fort Worth Museum of Science and History: planetarium

Cattle Raiser's Museum: exhibits and artifacts trace the changing face of the cattle trade

Modern Art Museum of Fort Worth: specializes in twentieth-century abstracts

Stockyards Collections Museum: cattle-market memorabilia

Cowtown Coliseum: presents regular rodeos

HILL COUNTRY

Fredericksburg

Pioneer Museum: made up of several original structures, including a church and a store

Admiral Nimitz Museum & Historical Center: incorporates the **Nimitz Steamboat Hotel**, once the last hotel on the military road to California; now holds a Museum of the Pacific War, a peace garden, and a historical trail that leads past aircraft, tanks, and heavy artillery

Lyndon B. Johnson National Historical Park

Preserves Johnson's birthplace and the ranch house where Lady Bird Johnson continued to live after her husband's death; a Living History Farmstead depicts German family life in the early 1900s

CENTRAL TEXAS

Austin

Capitol Complex: includes the *Texas State Capitol* (1888)

Governor's Mansion: constructed 1856; open for tours

Congress Ave. Bridge: home for a colony of Mexican free-tail bats

University of Texas Museums & Galleries: includes the *LBJ Library and Museum*; the *Texas Memorial Museum*, which displays Texas' natural and social history; and the *Archer M Huntington Gallery*, with a collection focusing on twentieth-century art, and drawings from the fifteenth century onward

Zilker Park: An 8-acre park with botanical garden, sculpture garden, and museum; access point to *Barton Springs* natural swimming pool, the *Barton Creek Greenbelt*, and the 60-acre *Zilker Nature Preserve*; also houses the *Austin Nature Center*

Mayfield Estate and Nature Preserve

Mount Bonnell: highest point in the city, panoramic views

National Wildflower Research Center: display garden featuring every type of wildflower and plant that grows in Texas

La Grange

Monument Hill Historical Park: burial ground for Texans who died in two major conflicts with Mexico in 1842

Kreische Brewery State Historical Site: provides guided tours of the ruins of one of Texas' oldest breweries

Hermes Drug Store: oldest in continuous operation in Texas

San Antonio

Paseo del Rio or *River Walk:* tropical plants and trees; passes *La Villita* ("little town"), San Antonio's original settlement

Buckhorn Hall of Horns, Fins and Feathers: at the *Lone Star Brewery;* a bar with exhibitions, and thousands of horns on display, as trophies, chandeliers, and chairs; there are also stuffed animals including "Blondie" the two-headed lamb

King William Historic District: elegant late-nineteenth-century homes of German merchants.

Institute of Texan Cultures: social history of thirty diverse cultures

Mexican Cultural Institute: displays of Mexican art

Tower of the Americas: observation deck at 750 feet

San Fernando Cathedral: the oldest in the United States

Spanish Governors Palace

Market Square: dates from 1840

McNay Art Museum: Houses the art collection of millionaire Marion McNay; includes New Mexico crafts, Gothic and medieval works, and Post-Impressionists

San Antonio Museum of Art: includes the Rockefeller Center For Latin American Art

San Antonio Missions National Historic Park: includes the *Alamo Mission*

The Mission Trail: runs 9 miles south along the river; four restored missions act as interpretive centers

EAST TEXAS

Big Thicket National Preserve

Contains huge variety of plant and animal life, including deer, alligators, armadillos, possums, hogs, and wildcat; over 300 species of birds; wildflowers, orchids, cacti, and yucca

Caddoan Mounds State Historic Site

Burial sites and reconstructed dwellings of the Caddo Indians, an early mound-building culture, active from the ninth to fourteenth centuries; includes videos on Caddoan history

Nacodoches

Caddo Indian Mound: ancient native dwelling

Sterne-Hoya House: oldest surviving and unreconstructed home in the town; illustrates early pioneer life

TOWARD THE PANHANDLE

Abilene

Grace Museum: displays of regional art, local history, and a children's museum

Center For Contemporary Arts: work by local artists

Paramount Theatre: tours of elaborate Moorish interior and showings of live theater productions, classic, and art films

THE PANHANDLE

Amarillo

Cadillac Ranch: ten battered roadsters stand upended in the soil

Livestock auction: regular tours of the stockyards

Canyon

Panhandle-Plains Historical Museum: exhibits on restored pioneer buildings, artifacts of the Plains Indians, the history of Texas ranching, natural history, and a collection of Western art

Lubbock

Ranching Heritage Center: over thirty original ranch buildings, from cowboy huts to overseers' houses; includes a museum on pioneer and cowboy history

Lubbock Lake Landmark State Historical Park: archaeological site with artifacts spanning 1,200 years

Prairie Dog Town: in Mackenzie State Park; home to some 600 prairie dogs

Llano Estacado Winery: guided tours and free tasting

Palo Duro State Canyon Park

Based in Palo Duro Canyon, with a depth of 1,200 feet; offers breathtaking views and colors

WEST TEXAS

Big Bend National Historic Park

Bordered by a section of the Rio Grande; million-acre expanse of pine-forested mountains and ocotilla-dotted desert; camping facilities available, but mostly barely chartered territory dotted with ruins of primitive Mexican and Anglo settlements

The River Road: runs through spectacular desert scenery for some 30 miles; passes through Lijitas and Terlingua

Santa Elena Canyon: challenging rafting route

Mexican side canyons: hiking trails in dramatic surroundings

Davis Mountains

McDonald Observatory: tours of the dome and 107-inch telescope provided; also hosts nocturnal "star parties" that provide the opportunity for visitors to view the constellations

Fort Davis National Historic Site: offers hiking, fishing, and swimming at the foot of a canyon in Limpia Creek

El Paso

Border Patrol Museum: explains the work of the border staff and highlights the ingenuity of smugglers

Tigua Indian Reserve: contains an arts and crafts center, selling pottery and textiles

Ysleta del Sur: the oldest mission in the United States; marks the beginning of a *Mission trail* that runs alongside cotton, alfalfa, chili, onion, and pecan fields

Guadalupe Mountains National Park

Offers hiking and camping with a trail to the top of Guadalupe Peak—the highest point in Texas at 8,749 feet

SOUTHERN TEXAS AND THE GULF COAST

Corpus Christi

South Texas Institute for the Arts: includes pieces by Monet and Picasso

Corpus Christi Museum of Science and Industry: specializes in hands-on natural history exhibits, with topics including hurricanes and naval aviation; also gives access to life-size replicas of the fleet of Christopher Columbus

Galveston

Texas Seaport Museum: focuses on the port's role in trade and immigration during the nineteenth century

Railroad Museum: steam trains, Pullman cars, and artifacts

Moody Gardens: a floral research facility with three giant glass pyramids—one holding exotic plants, birds, and fish from around the world; another housing a science museum; and the third holding an aquarium

Laredo

Republic of the Rio Grande Museum: local historical exhibits

San Augustin Plaza: the original Spanish settlement

Padre Islands National Seashore

Bird-watching, beachcombing, and camping

Houston

Museum of Fine Arts: oldest art museum in Texas with a large collection of French Impressionists, American Modernists, and Texan Postmodernists; also access to the sculpture garden, which contains works by Rodin

Contemporary Arts Museum: 10 or more temporary shows per year

The Holocaust Museum: permanent exhibition, housed in a black cylinder, traces the lives of European Jews from before World War II, through the Holocaust, and after the war

Hermann Park: 407-acre wooded park containing Houston Zoological Gardens

Museum of Natural Science: features a huge granite globe rotating in a fountain

Cockrell Butterfly Center: three-story dome containing thousands of live butterflies; also contains a natural history museum

The Orange Show: begun in 1954; a Jeff McKissack monument to honor the orange; started as a simple house, progressed to include sculptures, wishing wells, observation decks, and wheels, all painted orange

Museum of Printing History: rare and unusual printed works including the Dharani Scroll, which dates from 764 and is one of the oldest printed works in existence; also displays typography through the ages

Johnson Space Center: NASA center for planning and training

Space Center Houston: exhibits featuring *Faith-7*, the Mercury capsule used to orbit the earth; the command module from *Apollo 17*, used on the last trip by humans to the Moon in 1972; and a trove of Moon rocks; also contains Mission Control, the space shuttle training mock-up and zero-gravity labs

San Jacinto Battleground State Historical Complex: includes an elevator ride to the 489 foot high observation deck of the San Jacinto Monument; a museum displays a collection of historical Texas artifacts

NEVADA

Ely
Nevada Northern Railway Museum

Baker
Great Basin National Park:
Wheeler Peak; a six-story-high limestone rock formation; an ancient pine forest; prehistoric Fremont rock art; Lehman Caves

Eureka
Sentinel Newspaper Museum: original printing equipment and memorabilia from the 1800s
Tannehill Log Cabin: dated 1865, the first house in the town

Austin
A ghost town featuring *Stokes Castle*, an 1897 architectural oddity and exact replica of a tower outside Rome

Fort Churchill State Historic Park
Historic fort, built 1861 and partly restored with a visitor center

Virginia City
Mark Twain Museum: memorabilia from the newspaper days of the young author
The Way it Was Museum: mining history and artifacts
Gold Hill: preserved structures in a ghost town

Genoa
Mormon Station: museum of pioneer artifacts
Genoa Courthouse Museum: preserved courthouse and jail, now a museum of criminal history in the area
Genoa Bar: preserved 1850s bar, and the oldest saloon in the state

Berlin
Berlin-Ichthyosaur State Park: fossilized remains of three large ichthyosaurs
Diana Mine: tools and equipment; walking tours

Carson City
Nevada State Museum: housed in the 1869 Mint
Nevada State Railroad Museum: historic equipment
Stewart Indian Museum: housed in the 1890 intertribal boarding school; contains local memorabilia
Bowers Mansion: preserved nineteenth-century mansion of a wealthy prospector

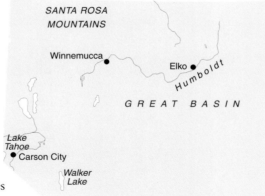

Reno
Morrill Mackay School of Mines Museum
Nevada Museum of Art: local artwork
National Automobile Museum: vintage and classic cars

Pyramid Lake
Scene of primitive beauty, with porous rock islands; visitor centers

Winnemucca
Humboldt Museum: local artifacts and a country store

Elko
Center of the largest cattle-ranching region in the nation; the *Northeastern Nevada Museum*, with regional historical exhibits and artifacts

Tonopah
Central Nevada Museum: artifacts and replicas of local interest; extensive outdoor exhibits, miners' cabins, and railroads

Rhyolite
Ghost town; maintains the *Las Vegas and Tonopah Railroad Depot*, and the well-known *Bottle House*, constructed of whisky bottles

Las Vegas
Well-known as the "entertainment capital of the world," with its legendary strip, four miles of casinos, and the most extravagant architecture of the twentieth century

Boulder City
Hoover Dam Museum: film of the dam's construction

Hoover Dam
Built between 1931 and 1936 and at that time the largest dam, at 726 feet high; tours available

Pioche
A ghost town and the most notorious mining camp in Nevada
Million Dollar Courthouse: built in 1871 at such expense that it was not paid off until 1937; a museum of local history
Valley of Fire State Park: contains Anasazi and Paiute petroglyphs; spectacular natural sandstone formations
Lost City Museum: reconstructions and artifacts of the largest Anasazi settlement in Nevada, 300 BC until 1150 AD
Red Rock Canyon: a 13-mile scenic drive through classic canyon scenery, often used as a movie setting

OKLAHOMA

EASTERN OKLAHOMA

Bartlesville

Price Tower: designed by Frank Lloyd Wright in 1956 with cantilevered stories resembling the branches of a tall tree

Frank Phillips Home: built in 1908 by the founder of Phillips Oil; an opulent display of wealth with elaborate interior decoration

Woolaroc Ranch: wildlife refuge and museum of Western art and history, containing over 60,000 artifacts; paintings; and decorative art, including Native American works and those of Remington and Russell

Claremore

The birthplace of humorist *Will Rogers*, and a shrine to him

Muskogee

Five Civilized Tribes Museum: tells the Native Americans' story through costumes, documents, photographs, and jewelry; also contains a reconstructed trading post and a print room

Lake Tenkiller: picturesque lake surrounded by woods, cliffs, and quiet beaches; offers fishing, boating, swimming, and scuba-diving, and has camping facilities

Tahlequah

Cherokee Heritage Center: presents Native American culture through historical artifacts including wooden ceremonial masks; a display covers the Cherokee alphabet; also contains a reconstructed seventeenth-century Indian village which gives arts and crafts demonstrations

Tulsa

Greenwood Historic District: features the *Greenwood Cultural Center*, which houses the *Goodwin-Chappelle Gallery*, a history of the district in photographs; and the *Oklahoma Jazz Hall of Fame*, a tribute to jazz greats, local and otherwise

Philbrook Museum of Art: a Florentine-style mansion with luxurious furnishings and design, and picturesque gardens with good hill views; displays include Native American pottery, African sculpture, Chinese jades, and Renaissance paintings

Gilcrease Museum: collection of Western art that includes Native American works, Remingtons, Russells, and Morans

Ted Allen Ranch: working horse ranch; activities include riding, overnight campouts, moonlit hayrides, and rodeos

OKLAHOMA CITY AND BEYOND

Guthrie

Guthrie Historical District: a collection of restored Victorian architecture

State Capitol Publishing Museum: exhibits printing technology from the earliest newspaper printed in Oklahoma Territory

Scottish Rite Masonic Temple: the largest Masonic complex in the world, featuring hundreds of bright stained-glass windows

Lazy E Arena: hosts world-champion rodeos and calf roping competitions

Oklahoma City

Myriad Gardens: landscaped with hills, gardens, and waterways; gives good views across to the brick-towered downtown skyline

Overholser Mansion: tours around the Victorian home

Oklahoma Heritage Center: local history and hall of fame

Enterprise Square USA: an outlandish area dedicated to consumer products, dollar bills, the government, and the economy

National Cowboy & Western Heritage Museum: combines fine and popular art; includes the works of Remington and Russell, contemporary Native American work, John Wayne's cowboy collection, and the Western Performers Hall of Fame, full of oil paintings and memorabilia; also includes Prosperity Town, the American Rodeo Gallery, and the American Cowboy Gallery

City Stockyards: live cattle auctions

Chickasaw National Recreation Area

There are exhibits, outdoor activities, nature walks, and camping available in this level landscape of cool streams and bromide and sulphur springs.

INDEX